The Theory and Ethnography of African Social Formations

THE THEORY AND ETHNOGRAPHY OF AFRICAN SOCIAL FORMATIONS
The Case of the Interlacustrine Kingdoms

Archie Mafeje

CODESRIA BOOK SERIES

The Theory and Ethnography of African Social Formations
The Case of the Interlacustrine Kingdoms

First published in 1991 by
CODESRIA BOOK SERIES
1 Ashdon Road, London NW10 3EH

CODESRIA is the Council for the Development of Economic and Social Research in Africa head-quartered in Senegal. It is an independent organization whose principal objectives are facilitating research, promoting research-bases publishing and creating multiple fora geared towards the exchange of views and information among African scholars. Its correspondence address is B.P. 3304, Dakar, Senegal.

ISBN 1 870784 08 1 (Paperback)
     1 870784 09 X (Hardback)

Cover designed by Bernard Canavan
Typeset by CODESRIA
Printed by RyanPrint, 1 Ashdon Road, London NW10 4EH
Distributors: ABC, 27 Park End Street, Oxford OX1 1HU

CODESRIA would like to express its gratitude to the Swedish Agency for Research Cooperation (SAREC), the Danish Agency for International Development (DANIDA), the Ford Foundation and the Norwegian Ministry of Foreign Affairs for Support of research activities and publication of the research results.

CONTENTS

To Shahida, Xolani and Dana

for our tribulations, triumphs and emancipation

ACKNOWLEDGEMENTS

Reflections on the themes pursued in this book began to take shape during my stay as a research fellow at the Institute of Social Studies, The Hague in 1983-1984. I am most grateful to the Rector and all the staff of the Institute for the opportunity. Contrary to the suppositions of bourgeois individualism, it is apparent that knowledge-making is truly a collective process. I benefitted greatly from the work of my European predecessors and associates including those whose theoretical outlook I do not share. I derived a great deal of inspiration from my African colleagues, especially those who came after me. Their impatience and readiness to denounce their would-be seniors as suffering from bourgeois hang-ups present one with a challenge, an audience to address and issues to clarify. Their insults are thus a great gift and give one a sense of relevance.

In moments of doubt one would have wished to check with one's cronies to avoid unnecessary risks. But in this age of jet-setting we are all too busy to read one another's manuscripts - a most regrettable fact. This might be one of the shortcomings of a young intellectual community which has no sense of investment through one another's work. Of my cronies, only Dr. Yash Tandon managed to take off time to read my manuscript. I need not say how much I appreciated his effort and cryptic remarks. These alerted me to certain conceptual problems, even if I was not able to resolve them. To Professor Peter Rigby, I am most grateful for his constructive and detailed criticisms.

Finally, I should like to express my sincere thanks to Safaa Youseef Sedky who cheerfully typed and re-typed the manuscript to its final form, without ever making me feel I was a burden on her. I could not help nick-naming her, "Smiling Beauty". Reem Saad Mikhail, my graduate assistant, had the thankless task of proof-reading the type-scripts and of compiling the bibliography - both finical and tedious jobs. For her patience and care I am most grateful. Naturally my debt to Shahida and Dana, who suffered long stretches of lack of family life while I busied myself seemingly interminably in my study, is inestimable.

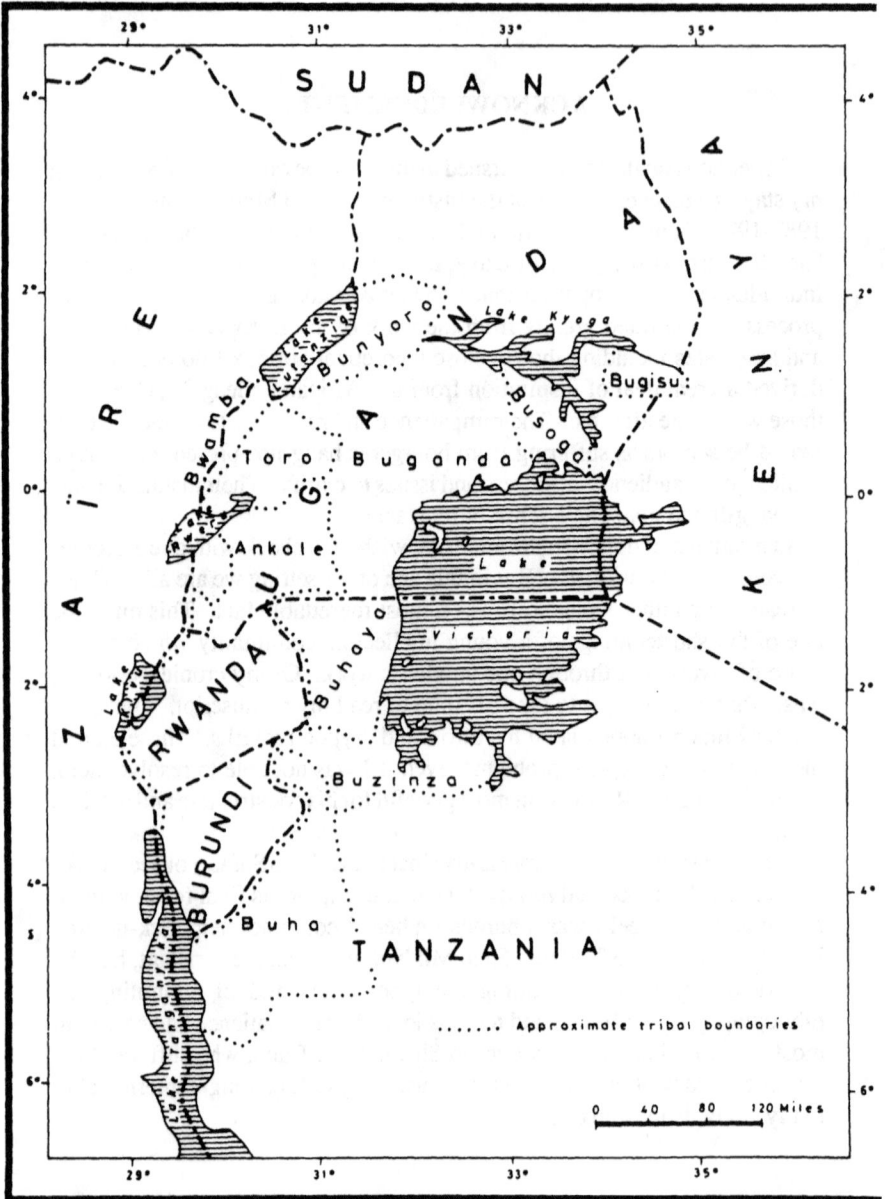

PREFACE

It is, perhaps, fair to state my own prejudices from the onset. Although I do academic work and believe in academic standards, I do not believe in erudition (which is another way of inhibiting the deprived or disadvantaged from writing what they know or think) and empiricism (which is a denial of the value of theoretical abstraction) as a mark of science. In my days as a science student at the University of Cape Town, for the required understanding of any phenomenon it sufficed to consult a few selected texts by recognized authorities in the field. Likewise, in scientific experiments replication was also finite i.e. infinity was reached after a given number of repetitions. Therefore, it may be asked of the social scientist: what is it that (s)he can hope to find in a multiplicity of texts and from an accumulation of "facts" which (s)he could not discover from a finite number of *strategically* selected texts and facts?

Lest it be thought that the comparison between social and natural sciences is unwarranted, we could refer to philosophy. When I got interested in epistemology, to acquire a good grasp of what positivism, Marxism, existentialism, or phenomenology is about, I did not have to read every text that had been written on anyone of them. A finite number of texts by the best exponents of each branch of knowledge sufficed. The same could be said of literary criticism. The essence is not the number of texts that one has read but how well one understands them.

There is no apparent reason why the so-called ideographic disciplines such as history, ethnography or anthropology should be any different. My starting point is that in theory-building significant differences do not occur at the level of "facts" but characteristically at the level of interpretation of "facts". This, correctly, presupposes that every professional practitioner has an adequate stock of information from which (s)he can make sustainable propositions. In normal scientific practice such information is standardized, only subject to individual emphases and refinement. In this way, certain schools get established and continue over time, without any dramatic changes. This set-up can only be disturbed by the discovery of new information which goes beyond the standardized or a new interpretation of the existing stock of facts in such a way that it acquires dramatically different connotations.

It is the latter that we are interested in. I believe that the first generation of European ethnographers in Africa produced very high quality monographs, most of which became classics in their own right. As would be expected, they got standardized, relying on certain fixed concepts such as "tribe", "lineage", "clan", etc., etc. But what facilitated the process even more was a search for taxonomic categories such as "acephalous" vs "centralized" states, "patrilineal" vs "matrilineal" societies, "pastoralists" vs "agriculturalists" etc., etc., which the famous anti-structuralist-functionalist British anthropologist, Edmund Leach, once contemptuously referred to as "butterfly collecting". Apart from the obvious organicism in structural-functionalist anthropology, taxonomic categories are by nature empiricist as well as static. Not only do they seek to put things in air-tight compartments but also, and more seriously, they substitute bounded forms for processes. This renders them utterly unhistorical. In this regard, it is interesting to note that in biology taxonomy has long been abandoned in favour of the more dynamic biochemical processes, which run through all forms of life and make them what they are. In human societies a number of social phenomena might appear as so many different *types*, only to discover that they are different *manifestations* or *permutations* of the same phenomenon, for example, modes of existence or social classification. This warns us against the pitfalls of both evolutionism and historicism. It is conceivable that there might never be a theory of mediations, but nonetheless mediations play a very important part in human history, as we hope to show.

My main concern in the present work is re-reading classical anthropological texts, in particular the *East African Chiefs*[1]. Unlike a number of more recent studies, the authors of *East African Chiefs* attempted a regional synthesis on the basis of what they thought were *common characteristics* (a taxonomic categorization). Seeing that they were Anglophone, they did not bother about the two French-speaking kingdoms in the region, Rwanda and Burundi. For these different texts had to be used. Reference is also made to more recent studies, especially by Ugandan historians. While they add to our stock of information, these studies do not seem to affect the classical paradigms. They use more or less the same designating categories and, perhaps, reach slightly different conclusions. Besides, ethnography or theory is not their main concern.

However, it is important to note that this is not necessarily true of all historians working on African societies. In *Modes of Production in Africa*[2] the authors made a serious effort to theorize African history. In fact, parallels could be drawn between what they were doing and what I propose to do. The difference is that they came with a given epistemology and an array of

---

1   Richards, A.I. (ed.), *East African Chiefs*, 1959.
2   Crummey, D. and Stewart C.C. (eds.), *Modes of Production in Africa*, 1981.

more or less taken-for-granted Marxist concepts such as "mode of production", "class", "economic surplus", "surplus value", "capitalist relations of production", and others. According to their own testimony, their intention was

> To demonstrate the pertinence, indeed the necessity for the application, of the concepts of historical materialism to the precolonial history of Africa[3].

There was also a stated desire to educate the Anglophone historians out of their "empiricism". There was no explicit wish to learn from the African ethnographies themselves but rather to extract as many historical "facts" as possible and interpret them according to certain preconceived categories.

I deliberately avoided all this. Using a discursive method, I allowed myself to be guided by the African ethnographies themselves. In trying to decode them, all pre-existing concepts became suspect and were subject to review. In the process a number of epistemological assumptions, including Marxist ones, ceased to be self-evident and became objects for intellectual labour, as Yash Tandon noted. In order not to be lost in a maze of theoretical texts, I chose one major text in exactly the same way I chose a particular set of classical ethnographic texts. This was Samir Amin's general thesis about *tributary modes of production* whose history, according to him, is outside the purview of European history. In other words, they could be understood in their own terms.

As somebody who is interested in the decolonization (or indigenization) of the social sciences, this appealed to me. I was not unaware of the dangers of relativized theory and sociological particularism. What proved to be most effective in resolving this problem was a totalizing *critique*. Having deciphered the chosen African ethnographies, I felt that I was in a position to evaluate them from inside outwards, i.e. towards the wider social environment, for example, colonial capitalism and struggles against imperialist domination.

Therefore, I set a great deal of store for the idea of "critique", for we are not asking to be praised but to be understood in our own terms. This granted, I am quite prepared to subject African societies, writers, and leaders to a scotching critique. This often raises questions about *empathy* in what is supposed to be inter-subjective communication. In this regard, one would like to refer to Peter Rigby's work. Rigby is probably the best among the

---

3   Op. cit. p. 11.

present generation of African ethnographers and certainly the ablest ethnolinguist amongst them. One has to read his *Persistent Pastoralists*[4] to appreciate this fully. Nonetheless, it is an affirmation, without negations. What starts off as a critique of the wider environment ends up as a phenomenological affirmation of the internal subjects. What of the inner system itself? Here, we encounter an apparent clash between critique and empathy. Need this be the case? As will be seen in the text, I am inclined to say "no", without detracting from brilliant ethnographic studies such as Rigby's.

Finally, as a matter of principle, I have whenever possible referred to people by the names they call themselves, without due regard for imposed orthographic conventions. For instance, instead of using noun stems only such as Nyoro, Ganda, and so on, I have retained the Bantu prefixes, *Mu* for singular and *Ba* for plural. The proper names thus become *Munyoro/Banyoro* or *Muganda/Baganda*. Similarly, for names of localities the original terms are used. Dubious terms such as "Hamitic" or "Nilotic" are used in inverted commas, if at all.

---

4   Rigby Peter, *Persistent Pastoralists*, 1985.

INTRODUCTION

Since the mid-1960s there has been a flush of literature on problems of "development", as against the neoclassical concept of "economic growth". This signified growing dissatisfaction with existing forms of practice and theory. However, the inability to find satisfactory solutions almost over a generation constituted an undeniable social and intellectual crisis. Historically, such ruptures have proved conducive to the growth of knowledge, if only because uncertainty leads to a ceaseless search for new answers. The desire for certainty may entail either the abandonment or radical revision of prevailing theoretical paradigms. In the absence of any dominant and pervading epistemology, the paths which this takes are often diverse and conflictive. This inevitably issues in theoretical incoherence which manifests itself in the mushrooming of a variety of "schools" which are often ephemeral.

While practitioners might agree on the existence of an intellectual crisis, they often differ as to its meaning and source. Nor does recourse to philosophy of science provide unambiguous answers. This has to be so because philosophers of science themselves are not agreed on whether intellectual crises lead to adjustments which are cumulative or to epistemological ruptures wherein preexisting paradigms are overthrown *in toto* and are replaced by new and incompatible ones. Likewise, there is no consensus among them as to whether the reasons for a general collapse are internal or external to extant theoretical frameworks. Advocates of "self-correcting" science such as Karl Popper maintain that the reasons are internal to the scientific enterprise itself and are, indeed, a logical outcome of the normal scientific process of "conjecture" and "refutation"[1]. This point of view is hotly contested by those philosophers who, like Thomas Kuhn[2], argue that science is not extra-societal and that, as such, its practice is conditioned by social factors which are exterior to it.

The latter position coincides with that of sociologists of knowledge which has been stoutly maintained by the members of the Frankfurt School, notably, M. Horkheimer, T. Adorno and J. Habermas. Its suppositions are derived from Marxist dialectics and historical materialism. But in their case

---

1   Popper, K., *Conjectures and Refutations*, London, 1963.
2   Thomas Kuhn, *The Structure of Scientific Revolutions*, Chicago, 1962.

it became so abstracted and divorced from current issues that it is ossified, even if brilliant and erudite in the classical sense. Without subscribing to any kind of "scientism" or suppositions about the inferiority of the social sciences, it must be admitted that the social sciences are particularly susceptible to their social and ideological environment. In fact, it may be stated quite categorically that lasting thought categories cannot but be reflective of contemporary social existence. In other words, social scientific questions are put on the agenda by current social struggles. This is not to deny the fact that social scientific pronouncements are not merely a reflection of reality but are also capable of projections which transcend the same reality. However, such transcendence is not a clear-cut process because rationalizations of any social phenomenon are subject to a range of background assumptions which are historically and culturally determined. Indeed, it is the duty of the theory of science to investigate and to reduce these into distinct epistemologies on which intellectual discourse is predicated. It is for this precise reason that in times of intellectual crisis there is (or there should be) recourse to questions of epistemology.

In the various controversies that have been raging within what is popularly known as "development theory", this condition has rarely been met. Terms such as "theory", "model" and "paradigm" and concepts such as "class", "mode of production" "social formation" and "economic surplus" are frequently involved, without due regard to their semantic status in theory and in practice. This has been particularly true of those approaches which have universalistic pretensions, for example, Gunder Frank's version of the *dependencia theory* and Immanuel Wallerstein's *world systems* analysis. The problem of reconciling universal history with local history is a vexing one, not so much analytically but mainly conceptually. Similar phenomena can be diagnosed all over the world. But the specific historical and social context in which they occur might make them hard to subsume under given general concepts, without distortion. In the social sciences, where the prospects for a meta-language are almost nil, the problem of translating from universal to *vernacular*[3] language cannot be minimized.

Put differently, the relationship between *ideographic* knowledge and *nomothetic* propositions is not an automatic one. This is so much so that, traditionally, a distinction had been made between ideographic and nomothetic disciplines. In the context of our impending study it is interesting to note that history and social anthropology had been identified

---

3   By "vernacular" is meant here ordinary common speech, as against learned speech.

with the former, whereas economics since the days of classical political economy had been treated as nomothetic. It was Marx who dispensed with the separation between economics and history by introducing dialectical materialism and historical materialism. Epistemologically, dialectical materialism did not recognize the division of knowledge into disciplines. It upheld not only the unity of knowledge but also the view that all scientific knowledge was reducible to finite nomothetic propositions or universal laws. In this context ideographic knowledge became a matter of detail or of so many forms which could be grasped by a single concept. Not only was this an historic challenge to positivism but was also a direct attack on the empiricist tradition within positivism. As a consequent, it is not uncommon among modern Marxists to abjure empirical studies and to treat abstract theory as superior knowledge. Yet Marx was not indifferent to specific studies, as is shown by his excitement about Morgan's *Systems of Consanguinity and Affinity of the Human Family* and the studies on the Russian commune. In contrast, his work suffered from lack of ideographic knowledge about non-European societies, especially the oriental societies about which he made unwarranted assumptions.

Of course, in theory, all Marxists vow that the only road to nomothetic propositions is through "the historically concrete". In practice, this could mean anything from Wallerstein's "world systems" analysis, Gunder Frank's and Samir Amin's "centre-periphery" trajectory, to Meillassoux's microcosmic studies of pre-capitalist societies in Africa. While attempts at making world wide generalizations might have helped to focus our attention on certain interconnections which had been obscured by the conventional approach of treating states or nations as units of analysis, truly universal concepts in the social sciences are rare and treacherous. At best, they are like skeletons, without flesh. It is, therefore, not surprising that Wallerstein's "world-systems" analysis has no distinct and really viable concepts. It is analogical in procedure. This has the effect of assimilating phenomena into one another and more or less ends up by affirming the old adage that "history repeats itself". Analytically, there is nothing objectionable about the use of analogies and metaphors. The only problem is that relations which have the same logical structure seldom function the same way in different historical contexts. If "world systems" are a dialectical unity, then its moments are subject to uneven changes and their implicit contradictions to non-recurrent mutations. In the light of this, historical specificity is the only medium through which world history can become comprehensible or acquire the necessary social relevance.

This raises questions about *authenticity* and interlocution which is both subjective and objective. We can all read world history but we can hardly be its universal agents in language and experience. For instance, everywhere nationalist movements seek to establish an identity other than the one ascribed to them by the world-system. In doing so they invoke vernacular language and make recourse to specific, local histories. These have to be understood in their own right in order to be decoded by any interlocutor. It is, perhaps, in this context that Gunder Frank's and Samir Amin's work received great resonance from the Third World. The division of the world into *centre* and *periphery* created grounds for affirming a *sui generis* identity for the Third World. They became effective interlocutors for Third World nationalism under conditions of imperialism. By revealing the objective negations of the imperialist "centre", they were able to affirm the unity of the underdeveloped "periphery". But when it came to regional specificities within the Third World itself, neither Frank nor Samir Amin was readily accorded the role of intellectual plenipotentiary for the region with which he was associated. In the case of Latin America *dependistas* such as Sunkel, Paz, Cardoso, Dos Santos and Fuenzalida felt usurped by Frank. They believed that he had perverted their perspective which was meant to explain, not the functioning of capitalism in its imperialist stage, but rather the similarities and differences in concrete situations of "dependency" in Latin America. Their project was mainly to elaborate an "historical model" for Latin America[4]. In Samir Amin's case, the Arab historians complained that he lacked detailed knowledge of the history of the region. On their part, the Africans complained that since his earlier work on Mali and the Maghreb, his writings on the rest of Africa had become impressionistic and yet he reserved the right to talk about "anything and everything authoritatively".

These strictures need not be interpreted as an overall rejection of the authors concerned. Writers such as Gunder Frank and Samir Amin still enjoy eminence in the Third World, if not elsewhere. But as all leaders, they are accountable. The question is: to what extent is their universalistic jargon reflective of the local "situations" or translatable into vernacular languages? Here, instances will vary, since they do not necessarily represent the same thing, methodologically. While Frank would not admit to being a Marxist of any description[5], Samir Amin, on the other hand, objects to being categorized as "neo-Marxist" and portrays himself as an "undogmatic" orthodox Marxist. True enough, big methodological differences are

---

4   See Villamil, J.J., *Transitional Capitalism and National Development: New Perspectives on Dependence*, Sussex, 1979, p. 44.

5   Frank, A.G., *Critique and Anti-critique: Essays on Dependence and Reformism*, N.Y., 1984, p. 258.

discernible in their works. Frank had been criticized on four major grounds: his notion of unit of analysis, substitution of exchange for production relations, the veracity of his ideographic propositions about Latin America and the validity of his global generalizations about the "periphery". On the question of what particular relations should be treated as determinate in the Third World countries, the most telling criticisms came from Laclau[6]. While not rejecting Frank's idea of a world capitalist-system divisible into "core" and "periphery" economies, Laclau suggested that participation in the capitalist systems should not be confused with the realization of the capitalist mode of production itself in underdeveloped countries. He maintained that *production*, not exchange, relations were the only reliable criterion for judging the nature of given economies.

Laclau's incisive remarks were immediately followed up by a more uncompromising attack from Arrighi[7]. His objections to Frank were not only to the fact that he had given a determinate role to exchange instead of production relations in his study of Latin American social formations but also to the fact that in his general analysis *class structure* got subordinated to colonial structure. Arrighi saw this as a form of historicism which militated against dynamic analysis as well as anti-imperialist struggles, since it attributed lack of development in Third World countries to a prior and unchanging cause. He further protested that in this way differences in class-structure in various ex-colonial societies and at different stages of their development could not be grasped. He charged that, instead, in Frank's work one is presented with an over-generalized postulate which lacks specificity both in historical time and in social content. On these grounds Arrighi was quite prepared to denounce Frank's outlook as "deterministic-ideological". Thereafter, many writers joined the fray, which reached its climax in the mid-seventies. The late seventies saw "the end of a debate". Many of Frank's followers felt that they had been led into a "cul-de-sac"[8]. Consequently, he was accused of "pessimism of the intellect" and "pessimism of the will"[9].

---

6   Laclau, H.E., *Feudalism and Capitalism in Latin America*, 1971.
7   Giovanni Arrighi, *The Relationship between the Colonial and the Class Structures: A Critique of Gunder Frank's Theory of the Development of Underdevelopment*, Dakar, 1971.
8   Browett, J.G., "Into the Cul de Sac of the Dependency Paradigm with A.G. Frank", *Australia and New Zealand Journal of Sociology, 1982.*
9   Bernstein, H. and Nicholas, H., *Pessimism of the Intellect, Pessimism of the Will*, Development & Change, 1983.

Although Frank rebutted these accusations point by point[10], he never quite succeeded in giving a systematic reply to the theoretical and methodological questions that had been raised against his approach or paradigm. After about twenty books he still had no recognizable corpus body of theory and distinct concepts. If his original intention was to demolish modernization theories which were imperialistic rationalizations and to demonstrate that since the days of colonialism there had been continued transfer of "economic surplus" from the underdeveloped to the developed countries, then his critique should have developed into a veritable theory of *imperialism*. This would have had to take into account the fact that there had been theories of imperialism before and that the "unequal exchange" which became so central in his work had already been identified by his predecessors in the Economic Commission for Latin America (ECLA). What might have proved an advantage to him is that the ECLA writers had not theorized the problem beyond neoclassical theories of growth as is implicit in his own distinction between "old" and "new" *dependencia*[11]. Second is the fact that existing theories of imperialism had been written from the point of the advanced countries, as is once again implied in his article "Real Marxism is Marxist Realism"[12]. Indeed, part of Frank's popularity derived from the fact that he wrote from the point of view of the underdeveloped countries. This gestalt shift actually produced a new paradigm whose historical significance should not be overlooked.

In our view, Frank's important paradigm collapsed within half a generation essentially because of lack of a new theory and new concepts to sustain it. Metaphors such as "development of underdevelopment", "metropolis"/"satellite", "lumpen bourgeoisie", "lumpen development", anecdotes and *ad hominem* polemics, once they had lost their initial appeal, were bound to rebounce because analytically they had very little value. First, imperialism is still thoroughly comprehensible in terms of exploitation of local labour by international capital, and not as a relationship between "proletariat" and imperialist nations. Second, while imperialist countries can be treated as identical, imperialism itself is a dynamic and highly adaptable phenomenon whose different stages are a problem of analysis and revolutionary strategy, and not of *status ante* arguments and fatalism. Third, while collectively victims of imperialism, underdeveloped countries vary

---

10   Op. cit., pp. 245-65.
11   Among the latter special reference is made to Laclau, Hinkelammernt, Glauser, Marini, and Torres.
12   Frank, A.G., *Real Marxism is Marxist Realism*, 1984.

greatly in class-structure and social age. Therefore, their terms of participation in the capitalist system vary accordingly. Recognition of this fact and emphasis on the political dimension of imperialism or anti-imperialism, as against the economistic or ethnocentric classical theories of imperialism which assumed that one way or the other underdeveloped countries would always play second fiddle to the advanced countries, would have been an important corrective.

For instance, Lenin assumed that revolutionary success in ex-colonial countries was contingent on the victory of the proletariat in the advanced capitalist countries. The Fourth International went so far as to deny the possibility of socialist revolution in backward countries in which the peasantry predominated. This presupposed the development of capitalism and the formation of an industrial proletariat, as happened in Europe. The implication was that underdeveloped countries were incapable of independent economic or political initiatives. Frank committed the same error by ascribing a passive role to underdeveloped countries which is determined by their dependence on the metropolitan countries. This leads to an underestimation of the anti-imperialist struggles in the Third World and the combative spirit of, at least, certain classes and fractions there. For that matter, "dependency" is not a country to country relation but rather a class relation. It is only certain classes in underdeveloped countries which get transnationalized and accept dependence because of the immediate gains they derive from it. Therefore, an analysis of the evolving class-structures in underdeveloped countries is of critical importance, theoretically and strategically. Frank's generalized category, "satellite", while asserting a certain unity at the universal level was ill-equipped to bring this out even for the specific region of Latin America.

The point here is that, while regions set certain socio-historical parameters, the analytical value of this is not fully realized until we have a deep appreciation of internal variations. Insistence on historical specificity is not a refusal to be analytically universal. It is one way of ensuring reliability and sensitivity of analytical tools in as much as it sets the range of their applicability. This is one of the lessons offered by the French *Annales*, the most successful school of social history. Comparative studies across regions must be more than analogies. They must be informed by local history. If the questions that are being raised are the same, regional specializations can only be an asset, seeing that as individual scholars we cannot hope to command the vernaculars and histories of all peoples of the world. These can be deciphered only through authentic local interlocutors. This is consistent with struggles for national or regional liberation, with calls for the indigenization of the social sciences and with the rejection of homogenization of all social existence under the pretext of "universalism". This is, perhaps, what the *dependencia* approach was meant to promote in Latin America before it was "perverted" by Frank, as is alleged by its originators.

In the last decade and a half we have seen similar efforts in the Indian sub-continent which culminated in what became known as the "Indian Debate". No particular paradigm has emerged from the Indian subcontinent, but very few are unaware of what concepts do not fit the complexity of the region. All these regional experiences or perspectives have universal implications in so far as they enhance our intellectual awareness by drawing our attention to the unfamiliar. Whatever parallels or distinctions are drawn from them are less likely to be a misinterpretation or an insensitive imposition. Traditional notions about generalizations being the hallmark of science make it difficult to accord the same status to dissimilarities as to similarities. Yet, it is apparent that dissimilarities in contemporary societies might facilitate our intellectual development by providing us simultaneously with a variety of social laboratories. For instance, Europe, which has for the last three hundred years looked upon technology as the solution to all problems, can at this juncture answer conclusively the question of what is the relationship between social development and technological development. Asia, which has had experience with large-scale societies which were able to reproduce themselves over a long period, without developing private property or accumulation of capital stocks, might give us better clues about socialist organization than advanced capitalism. Despite Marx, it cannot be purely accidental that the only *popular* socialist revolutions the world has seen so far took place there. For those who think in terms of institutions and culture, Latin America which, like North America, was a locus of transfer of European institutions and culture, became a perfect example of a counter theory to modernization theories which was of benefit to the other underdeveloped regions as well. In a world which is dominated by classical theories of agrarian societies and definitions of "peasants", Africa holds good prospects for transforming all such theories or definitions.

It is with this conviction that the present study is undertaken. As such, its main objective is a methodological and theoretical review of what had gone on before in African studies. At its most general level, it is a critical comment on the increasing separation between nomothetic propositions and ideographic knowledge. This has been manifest especially among the left. Although no absolute statements can be made, "world-systems" analysis and "centre"/"periphery" global suppositions suffered to varying extents from this tendency. Lack of clear units of analysis led to excessive use of analogies and metaphors, instead of rigourously defined concepts. At the intermediate level, the study is a comment on how particular disciplines such as anthropology, history and economics in Africa, by engaging in atomistic studies, failed to see the trees for the wood. While their concepts were often rigourously defined, they were so narrow and overlaiden with alien presuppositions that they failed to capture the totality of the social existence of the communities under study. Our prime example is the concept of "tribe". Were all African social formations "tribal"? Was the history of Africa necessarily a history of "tribes"? Was there something called "tribal economy" or "communal property" in land in Africa? Rank empiricism, like universalism, can lead to very serious misconceptions or distortions.

At its most fundamental level the study aims at reconceptualizing a number of social phenomena and social relations in black Africa which had been looked upon in certain ways, largely by non-Africans. The intention is to show that most of these had been misconceptions which are attributable to an inarticulation between universal language, as is employed in the social sciences and derived from European historical experience, and vernacular, as is experienced and understood by the Africans themselves. As we see it, what is at issue is the authenticity of social science texts. Our belief is that in the social sciences there are no texts, without a historical context. Therefore, in order to be able to decode certain texts, the interlocutor must have a deep understanding of their historical context. The argument here is not that social formations are determined by the ethnographies which accompany them but that ethnographies provide codes for conduct, social classification and ideological reproduction. The same class category need not behave the same everywhere in the world. African entrepreneurs might forgo opportunities to maximize value in favour of kinship considerations or leisure. In Buganda landlord-chiefs found greater value in political followers than in servile labour. For evaluating prospects for development, all these reflexes are relevant and valid, which is not to say they are objective. It is important to bear in mind that vernaculars, like all languages, are capable of illumination as well as mystification. Appreciation of what is involved contextually is what saves the analyst from being misled. In decoding vernaculars it is not as if we are reading off what is self-evident. This is the precise fault of both the empiricists and self-styled universalists. "Decoding" normally means expert translation from an obscure language into a more intelligible one. Therefore, in insisting on the comprehension of the vernaculars, we are not proposing to jettison the more general social scientific language. Our only demand is that it be informed by local expertise and, thus, endowed with greater validity and objectivity. From the point of view of social theory, this involves a process of sifting, discarding and recasting.

Among those who have been concerned to develop radical social theory in Africa and elsewhere, Samir Amin has carved a special position for himself. While he cannot be recommended for his disregard for detail and intellectual impetuosity which issues in bold and often metaphorical assertions, he is certainly to be commended for his critical intellect and ceaseless quest for new meanings. Notwithstanding the fact that most of these meanings had not been substantive but largely logico-deductive, they required of him greater rigour than is found among his associates such as Frank and Wallerstein. Here, we have in mind his work on dialectics, modes of production and social formations. These have been used in the present study as a point of departure. In that sense the study is a critique as well as an appreciation of Samir Amin's work in this particular domain. This is especially true of his "tributary mode of production", his concept of "social formation" and particular version of historical materialism, pertaining to "necessary" stages of development. It is also an indirect intervention in the polemics he has had with French Marxist anthropologists such as Godelier and Meillassoux. It would seem that, irrespective of whatever prejudices Samir Amin might have against anthropologists, researchers such as Meillassoux and his followers must be taken seriously. Their work is the best attempt thus far to reconcile Marxist analytical categories with vernaculars in pre-capitalist societies. Their deep ideographic knowledge, far from diminishing their capacity to produce nomothetic propositions, has helped them to generate new concepts, without being eclectic. Indeed, part of our inspiration is drawn from Meillassoux's work which marks a radical departure from traditional anthropology, as will be seen in the main text.

Although the title of the book refers to African social formations, in actuality the book deals with the interlacustrine kingdoms in East Africa, an area in which I did field work in the mid-1960s and in which I lived in the early 1970s. The only reason for the more general allusion to Africa is that the questions dealt with in the interlacustrine kingdoms are believed to be applicable to the different regions of sub-Saharan Africa. It is also an expression of a desire for similar work to be done in these other regions so as to confirm or refute our suppositions. Even so, we have been very careful not to generalize our findings beyond confirmed cases. We have, thus, left room for unexplored theoretical possibilities, especially in West Africa - a most complex and fascinating region in black Africa.

The main text of the book is divided into five chapters (II-VI). Chapter II deals with broader questions about *ethnography*, which have nothing to do with "ethnic" or "tribal" identities. It is argued that this approach opens up new possibilities which had been denied by classical anthropology. Secondly, it attempts to redefine the concept of *social formation*, with the intention of negating the definition adopted by Samir Amin and other "articulation" theorists. Chapter III deals with modes of political organization. Latter-day political economists and orthodox Marxists might object to the separation of politics from economics. But after due consideration based on material evidence we came to the conclusion that the relationship between modes of political organization and modes of economic production is not absolute but relative. The interlacustrine kingdoms exhibited the same mode of production but were at different stages of centralization of political power. In Chapter IV, which deals with economic organization, it is apparent that the politics of pastoralism manifested themselves in a slightly different from that in the agricultural kingdoms. But the most important point about Chapter IV is the absence of property and labour-relations in what is presumably class societies. This forces questions on us about what is meant by "class" in different contexts. Chapter V deals with the problem of modes of production and is concerned in particular to test Samir Amin's suggestive concept of "tributary mode of production". Chapter VI is largely a reflection on the findings of the study and leads to the necessary modifications and eliminations. As its title suggests, it is slightly speculative or contemplative. The opportunity for checking some of the hunches developed in the study is provided in Chapter VII, which deals with the reaction to colonialism in Buganda and its after-effects. This raises questions about underdevelopment and the historical necessity of capitalism or socialism in ex-colonial countries.

Finally, it is important to note that this study is not meant to be definitive but rather exploratory. It is a search for new definitions of African social formations. In order to arrive at this, a re-evaluation of pre-existing paradigms became essential. This entailed treating certain classical paradigms as standard or representative. In other words, individual variations were seen as detail within given paradigms. Consistent with this, the review of the literature is not exhaustive and had not been intended to be so as to facilitate and to concentrate the effort to overthrow particular paradigms. In this regard the genre of texts is more important than their volume. Likewise, refinements within the same pervasive paradigms have not been allowed to detract from the fundamental objective of the study, namely, to overthrow the paradigms themselves.

THE ETHNOGRAPHY AND SOCIAL FORMATIONS OF THE INTERLACUSTRINE

Some years ago it would have been inconceivable to think of the ethnography of the various peoples inhabiting the interlacustrine region in the singular. Traditional anthropology thrived on unravelling ethnographic details and peculiarities of particular tribes or peoples. Originally the term *ethnography*, as attested to by the English dictionary referred to "the scientific description of races of men". It was, therefore, barely distinguishable from ethnology which was thought of as a "science of races and their relation to one another and characteristics". The idea of human varieties and their possible classification is revealing. But it is fair to point out that in its modern usage the term, "ethnography", has a stronger social and cultural referent than a racial one. The major pre-occupation of the modern ethnographers is to isolate detailed patterns of social and cultural organization of given peoples or communities. Even so, the intention to establish taxonomic categories persists.

Although once very popular in anthropological literature, taxonomic classifications are rather a primitive, if natural, way of comprehending the world. Not only do they introduce discontinuities where none exist, but also mistake forms for processes. As a reaction against this, it would be silly to suppose that different forms might not connote different processes or qualities. The crux of the matter is how to conceptualize differences or similarities in quality, without being distracted by variations in form. In this context it is noteworthy that it was precisely the similarity in form among the *interlacustrine* kingdoms which struck anthropologists most rather than the ethnographic unity of the people who constituted themselves into such kingdoms. There was thus an apparent contradiction between unity of forms and ethnographic diversity which led to unnecessary speculation and controversies verging on racism.

Anthropologists and explorers alike identified a number of tribes in the interlacustrine region. To assert ethnographic unity in the face of such diversity of tribes is, thus, a contradiction in terms. But what is at stake is precisely the revision of these terms. First, it may be posited that ethnography is the study of a complex of socio-cultural relationships which can manifest themselves in a variety of forms, without losing their basic unity. It must be stressed that ethnography has nothing to do with race or ethnic origin but rather with learnt habits. First and foremost among these is language, which is the medium for social and cultural creativity. This perspective fits the interlacustrine people perfectly. As Audrey Richards testifies:

> These peoples of Uganda, Tanganyika and Rwanda-Urundi are linguistically akin. Luganda and Lusoga fall into one group, while Runyoro, Rutoro, Luhaya and Luzinza form a second, and the languages of the Rwanda, Rundi and Ha fall into a third[1].

However, she submits that "these tribes were initially grouped together ..... on basis of their political organization"[2], namely, centralized kingdoms.

In the last statement we witness the usual conflation by anthropologists between "tribe" and linguistic group. Nevertheless, if the term "tribe" refers to a specific form of political organization, then ethnographic evidence from Africa indicates that this need not coincide with linguistic boundaries. People who speak the same language may be divided into a number of independent chiefdoms or tribes. In the interlacustrine region we have examples of this, as is acknowledged in the introduction to *East African Chiefs*:

> Others (tribal systems) were multi-kingdom tribes, composed, that is, of a series of small principalities, each with its own hereditary ruler. Busoga, Buhaya, Buzinza and Busukuma were of this type ....[3].

Conventional anthropologists such as Audrey Richards and her collaborators were not equipped to deal with the theoretical implications of such an historical reality. Hence, they were reduced to employing such ambiguous characterizations as "multi-kingdom tribes". On the reverse side, there are cases such as Bunyoro, Ankole, Rwanda and Burundi where unitary kingdoms flourished, despite apparent ethnographic diversity. The latter appears to be so only because anthropologists often associated ethnography with particular ethnic groups. Thus, the co-existence of the Bairu and Bahima in Bunyoro and Ankole or of the Bahutu and Batutsi in Rwanda and Burundi constituted something of an anomaly. This was in spite of the fact that in all four cases the founding peoples produced an interesting socio-cultural amalgam.

---

1   Richards, A.I., *East African Chiefs*, London, 1959; pp. 27-28.
2   Op. cit., p. 28.
3   Op. cit., p. 14.

We have asserted that ethnography is independent of race or ethnic origin. Here, there are two main points at issue. First, it is conceivable that the same people can in different epochs be subjects of different ethnographies. In the event they might be referred to by different names. Second and most important for our purposes, is the possibility that, owing to circular migration within a given area, the same generic stock and within the same epoch might account for ethnographic variation. This might be a result of adaptation to varied ecological conditions or contact with other peoples. As will be adduced later, the interlacustrine Bantu-speakers, who are known by different tribal names and who belonged to distinct political entities at particular times, are a case in point. Even the distinctness of such entities should not be exaggerated, as they were all subject to continual processes of fusion and fission which made them more than bounded tribal units. The idea of cultural continuity and reproduction of the same political model on a limited or expanded scale is suggestive. Seen in its historical context, it means that the interlacustrine peoples had ceased to see themselves as only isolated, kin-based groups. Indeed, since the rise of Bunyoro-Kitara in the 15th century, the history of the region is but one of ruling dynasties, seeking to impose their authority over wider and wider areas often inhabited by people whose culture, language and modes of social organization were not dissimilar (see below). This observation has far-reaching theoretical implications, among which is the question of what is meant by "society" and how its boundaries are determined.

This brings us face to face with our second chosen concept, *social formation*. Conventional anthropologists or ethnographers habitually talk about societies not only as self-evident units but also as bounded systems. In their case ethnography largely coincides with "society". In contrast, Marxists have long rejected the concept of "society" as unscientific or ideological and have substituted, instead, the concept of "social formation", which has been given a new currency by Balibar's work. As Balibar puts it:

> ... the term 'social formation' which Marx uses, may be either an empirical concept designating the object of a concrete analysis, i.e., an *existence* ... or else an abstract concept replacing the ideological notion of 'society' and designating the object of the science of history in so far as it is a totality of instances articulated on the basis of a determinate mode of production[4].

---

4   Althusser, L. and Balibar, E., *Reading Capital*, London, 1970, p. 207.

Balibar's first definition has been used with reference to black Africa by writers such as Samir Amin and Rey. For Amin,

> ... social formations are *concrete* structures, organized and characterized by a *dominant* mode of production which forms the apex of a complex set of subordinate modes of production[5].

Here, we encounter the beginnings of the so-called theory of "articulation of modes of production", which got fuller expression in Rey's work[6]. In his definition Rey emphasized not only the articulation between modes of production but also the combat between them and all the confrontations and alliances it implies. It would be inappropriate at this stage to enter into a detailed discussion of these definitions, but it should suffice to note that they are an important point of departure for those who use the concept of "social formation".

Accordingly, it is our intention in the present study to check the empirical and theoretical validity of these definitions. Our working hypothesis is that social formations refer to something other than articulation of modes of productions. The main reason for this pre-supposition is that, if social formations are concrete structures or articulations, then they cannot have modes of production, which are by general consensus *abstract*, as their constituent elements. In its concrete form the economic instance is comprehended only at the level of production, and not at the level of abstract, synthetic concepts. Likewise, in its concrete form the combat or class struggle between representatives of competing modes of production referred to by Rey is grasped only at the level of social relations and their reproduction. This may be referred to as the instance of power which guarantees social reproduction through political struggles and ideological affirmations. In our view, it is the articulation between the economic instance and the instance of power which comprises the *social formation* of any society. Not only is this concrete in its reference and exhaustive of all forms of social discourse (praxis), but it is also universal in its application. The weakness of Rey's definition was that it did not apply to societies with a single mode of production such as the United States. Samir Amin's conception suffered from the same weakness as well as from a certain illogicality in so far as it derived concreteness from an articulation of abstract modes of production which, as Balibar warns, are not to be confused with

---

5   Amin Samir, *Underdevelopment and Dependence in Black Africa: Historical Origins,* 1972, p. 107.
6   Rey, P. - P., *Les Alliances des Classes*, Paris, 1973.

historical instances or real existence. Both the value of Balibar's injunction and the significance of our notion of ethnography and social formation can best be illustrated by a concrete analysis of the history of the interlacustrine peoples.

THE INTERLACUSTRINE REGION AND ITS PEOPLES

The interlacustrine region, as the term implies, is an area which is encircled by the great East African lakes of Victoria, Kyoga, Albert, Tanganyika, George, Edward and Kivu. These marked out a particular ecological zone, which is limited in the west by the Central African rift valley from Lake Tanganyika to Lake Albert, in the north and east by lakes Kyoga and Victoria, and in the south by a line running westwards from Lake Victoria to the Malagarasi River. Within this vast area of about .... square kilometres lived Bantu-speakers who were divided into ten main kingdoms - Bunyoro, Toro, Buganda, Busoga, Ankore, Buha, Buhaya, Buzinza, Rwanda and Burundi. In terms of political organization the only exceptions were Bwamba, Rwenjura and Kigezi which had been described by anthropologists as segmentary or acephalous societies due to their lack of centralization. Ethnographically, it is important to note that *lineages*, to which the term *segmentary* refers, persisted as a form of political organization at the local level even in the centralized kingdoms. It is apparent therefore that all these societies were in transition from one form of political organization to another. The anthropological dichotomy between *acephalous* and centralized "states" tended to obscure this historical process.

Nor should this be viewed in an evolutionary way. All segmentary societies in the region were not destined to become centralized kingdoms but rather were exposed to centralizing tendencies. This was the case in Bunyoro-Kitara, Ankore, Buhaya and Rwanda where the original, decentralized, agricultural communities were imposed upon by empire-building pastoralists who came from outside. For this to happen, the empire-builders need not have come from outside as is exemplified by the case of Buganda, Busoga and all the other Bantu kingdoms, stretching from the Congo through Zambia, Zimbabwe and down to South Africa. The rise of certain clans and lineages to political eminence and their establishment as royal clans and ruling dynasties is more characteristic of the Bantu-speakers from at least the 15th century onwards than anything else. In fact, most of the anthropological studies on kingdoms come from this part of Africa. Secondly, pastoralism is common among those Bantu-speaking communities which settled in tsetse-free zones. Therefore, the distinction between pastoralist invaders and native agriculturalists is, historically, not diagnostic. Furthermore, the so-called *Hamitic* pastoralists of the north were, historically, the epitome of segmentary societies. The acephalous societies of the anthropologist referred to them almost without exception[7]. The question of why and how in moving south they, all of a sudden, became founders of powerful kingdoms has to be explained, sociologically and not racially. In passing it is worth noting that, though speculation about their origin went as far afield as pre-dynastic Egypt which was not pastoralist anyway, the long-horn cattle which are associated with the Huma/Hima pastoralists are found not only in southern Somalia and Ethiopia but also in the north of Sierra Leone, along River Niger and as far south as Namibia. Therefore, neither the geographical distribution of the cattle nor the supposed racial origins of the pastoralists gives us any clues as to the rise of kingdoms in the interlacustrine region.

THE INTERLACUSTRINE SOCIAL FORMATIONS

As has been mentioned, by the end of the 19th century the people of the interlacustrine region were divided into ten main kingdoms and three segmentary societies. They all spoke Bantu languages. The kingdoms, though ruled by dynasties of supposedly different ethnic origins, bore great resemblance to one another in their constitutions. However, some consisted of an admixture of peoples, for example, Bunyoro, Ankore, Rwanda, Buhaya, Buha and Buzinza, whereas some showed great homogeneity, for example, Buganda and Busoga. This has given rise to a problem of class and caste in the interlacustrine social formations. From the point of view of political economy, class and caste are relative terms. But from the point of view of ethnography, they might not be. Therefore, there is a point to prove in our analysis of the processes of state-formation among the interlacustrians. Chronologically, it would appear that the kingdoms that exhibited caste formations were earlier, whereas those which exhibited mainly class were later. Whether this is a coincidence or the logic of historical development is a matter which should await further investigation. For the time being, we propose to start with the heterogeneous formations.

Heterogeneous Formations

There are obvious affinities and resemblances among the heterogeneous formations of Bunyoro, Ankore, Rwanda, Burundi, Buhaya, Buha and

---

7   See Middleton, J. & Tait, D., *Tribes Without Rulers*, London, 1958.

Buzinza. But any attempt to evolve an ordered history of the rise of these kingdoms meets with difficulties at every turn. First, the early history of these societies, which is unrecorded, is shrouded in mystery and legend. The early recorded accounts by European explorers and ethnologists such as Speke, Baker and Roscoe often substituted fantasy for facts, largely because of lack of respect for indigenous oral historians. In the other direction oral traditions on which anthropologists and post-independence nationalist historians rely often resort to hero-worshipping as a claim to fame and antiquity. This is apparent in the work of the present generation of Ugandan historians such as Kiwanuka[8] and Karugire[9]. Yet, if critique is the objective of our inquiry, it must be an impartial one. More specific references are made in the next section of this chapter.

It is evident that the first known processes of political centralization occurred in Bunyoro. Using genealogical charts of ruling dynasties and other known episodes, this falls somewhere in the 15th century. The actual date is immaterial as the social age of a society has very little to do with chronology. In their oral traditions the Banyoro acknowledge three ruling dynasties: first, the shadowy Tembuzi, then, the mysterious Chwezi hero-gods and, finally, the Babito to whom the modern Bunyoro monarchs trace their descent. The big puzzle here is that there is no mention of the Bahuma (Bahima elsewhere in the region) dynasty and none of the authorities who took the traditional Bunyoro version at its face value are able to fit the Bahuma into this scheme of things. They merely refer to the existence of a Bahuma aristocracy which is believed to be of "Hamitic" origin by virtue of its physical appearance. The following passage form Beattie's book is typical and has been uncritically received by a number of writers on Bunyoro:

> Throughout this region the pastoral Hima invaders (called Huma in Bunyoro) assumed the role of overlords, dominating the indigenous Iru, or peasant peoples, who form the governed majority. But for Bunyoro this is an oversimplification. Although the cattle-herding Huma have always regarded themselves as superior to Iru, in Bunyoro the matter was complicated many generations ago by the arrival from the north of the Nile of a third element, the Bito, whose affinities are with the non-Bantu

---

8   See Kiwanuka, S., *A History of Buganda from the Foundation of the Kingdom to 1900.* London, 1971.
9   Karugire, S., *A History of the Kingdom of Nkore in Western Uganda to 1896*, Oxford, 1971.

Acholi and Alur of present-day Uganda. These darker-skinned "Nilotic" invaders took over the Nyoro Kingship from an earlier dynasty, and the present Mukama claims to be the twenty-sixth Bito king. Much of the prestige and authority associated in the more southerly kingdoms of the region with the Hima attaches in Bunyoro to the Bito ...[10].

As will be noticed, Beattie does not specify from which dynasty the darker-skinned "Nilotic" invaders took over the Bunyoro kingship. But, instead, he slides into the same position as the present kings of Bunyoro. The only way we can credit the story of three dynasties in the history of Bunyoro is to suppose that it was the Chwezi kings who were chased out by the Babito invaders. If we assume, as we must, that the Bachwezi were part of the Bahuma invasion, then everything would be thrown into relief and they would cease being so mysterious. In being driven out of Bunyoro the Bahuma dynastic pastoralists would have been inclined in a south-westerly direction where ecological conditions are ideal for cattle-herding. In the event their reappearance as conquering Bahima herders in Ankore, Rwanda and Burundi, and spreading across to Buhaya, Buha and Buzinza becomes explicable. This also fixes their movements in time. If their date of arrival in Bunyoro falls somewhere in the 15th century and they remained in the area for a "few generations", then most of the southward-bound movement must have occurred during the 16th century. Using names of actual known kings of Rwanda, (thirty-one generations), Maquet reaches the same conclusion[11].

There is one more puzzle to solve. Oral traditions from Bunyoro are utterly ambiguous on the question of the origins of the Bachwezi. One account gives the distinct impression that the Bachwezi kings were a result of ascendancy from within, for Ndahura, the first Muchwezi king, usurped his grandfather Bukuku's throne, - a commoner who fortuitously fell into power and whose daughter, Nyinamwiru, unknown to him, had been cohabiting with the son of the former king to beget Ndahura. Putting aside the convulsions of the story, what is clear is that it denotes the ascendancy to power from among the original Bairu inhabitants. Indeed, the name "Nyinamwiru" means mother of Mwiru (singular of Bairu).

In contradistinction, the Bachwezi are said to have come from very far away. If they are the ancestors of the present Bahuma, then their somatic type will confirm the latter story and make nonsense of the first. Secondly,

10   Beattie, J., *Bunyoro, An African Kingdom*, N.Y., 1960, p. 3.
11   Maquet, J., *The Premise of Inequality in Rwanda*, London, 1961, p. 12.

if the original inhabitants were agriculturalists, then we have to explain the introduction of cattle-herding which became so predominant among the rulers of Bunyoro. It could be easily assumed that they came with the Babito. But then how would we explain the existence of the Bahuma pastoralists further south in Ankore, Burundi and Rwanda where the Babito invaders did not go and the presence of a light-brown, presumably half "Hamitic" stock in Bunyoro and Toro? The obvious solution would be to discount the likelihood of the ascendancy of the original agriculturalists to royalty in Bunyoro. In the circumstances the introduction of pastoralism as an elite pursuit must be attributed to the "Hamitic" invaders who, probably, migrated from south-eastern Ethiopia and southern Somalia with their long-horned cattle.

This does not mark the end of unsolved puzzles about the early history of Bunyoro. While it is generally agreed that, whoever the Bachwezi were, they were definitely succeeded by the darker-skinned Luo-speakers from north of the Nile, the Banyoro oral traditions do not associate the latter with pastoralism either. Beattie reports that:

> When the Bito first arrived in Bunyoro, they seemed strange and uncouth to the inhabitants ... they had to be instructed in the manners appropriate to rulers; at first they were ignorant of such important matters as cattle keeping and milk drinking. But gradually Rukidi assumed the values and manners proper to the heir of the pastoral rulers of the earlier dynasties. So began the reign of the powerful dynasty Bito which has lasted up to the present[12].

How so? The Luo-speakers are by tradition pastoralists. It is unlikely that they were ignorant of cattle-keeping. But it is most likely that they were ignorant of the kingship institutions which in Bunyoro centred on sacred herds and a milk diet for the kings. This is not surprising if it is recalled that, historically, the Luo-speakers are not associated with kingship but rather with lineage organization. Neither are the "Hamitic" pastoralists associated with kingdoms. The question then is: why are both groups of pastoralists supposed to have established kingdoms on entering the interlacustrine region?

At least, three basic considerations can be entertained here. First, for the purposes of state-formation, a settled population is necessary for both production and for raising revenues. In Bunyoro and elsewhere in the interlacustrine region the Bairu agriculturalists met this condition.

---

12   Beattie, J., op. cit., p. 15.

Secondly, it is apparent that while land was over-abundant among the agriculturalists, cattle were not. In fact, once introduced, the cattle became a prestige good *par excellence* and became surrounded with all sorts of royal rituals. In Bunyoro there were sacred royal herds which provided milk for the king. Who ever had large herds of cattle was assured of an elevated social status. In this respect the Luo cattle-herders had an advantage over the Bairu cultivators. Thirdly, the mystique and prestige attached to cattle were enough to give the pastoralists a privileged position. If so, they did not have to conquer the cultivators but merely to exploit their sensibilities. Indeed, the Bachwezi became the hero-gods of the Banyoro. It is not unusual in African oral traditions for those who brought with them valued assets, be they cattle, fire or iron, to be endowed with god-like attributes. From this combination of objective and subjective factors, it would not be unreasonable to suggest that neither the Bairu nor the pastoral immigrants take credit for the development of kingship in Bunyoro. It was rather the dialectical interaction between the two. The Bairu provided the agricultural base and services and the pastoralists, relieved of any onerous duties but in control of prestige goods, indulged themselves, turned the latter into a mechanism for political control and ritual mystification. This phenomenon, involving the same social categories, got repeated in five other kingdoms in the interlacustrine region - Ankore, Burundi, Rwanda, Buhaya and Buzinza. We encounter here an integration of the economic instance with the instance of political power, despite the co-existence of two distinct modes of existence - pastoralism in the hands of the Bahuma and agriculture in the hands of the Bairu. This is no mere division of labour or mixed farming, as we are accustomed to among the Bantu-speakers farther south[13]. Individuals might have crossed political boundaries, as Beattie assures us[14], but this did not represent an assimilation of one mode of existence into the other. The two modes provided a basis for status as well as class distinctions. It would be convenient to regard this as a transient phenomenon. But such facile suppositions are contradicted by the case of Ankore, Burundi and Rwanda, where it persisted for centuries.

As is well-known, on reaching Bunyoro the Bahuma did not give up altogether their nomadic pastoralism. Some continued in a south-westerly direction and established themselves as overlords in Ankore, Rwanda and Burundi, where they are known as Bahima and Batutsi, respectively. Once again, they imposed themselves on Bantu-speaking agriculturalists, the

13   See Schapera, I., (ed.), *The Bantu-speaking Tribes of South Africa*, London, 1937.
14   Richards, op. cit., pp. 100-1.

Bairu in Ankore and the Bahutu in Burundi and Rwanda. As roving bands in foreign territory, the Bahuma must have been prepared for the worst, militarily. Yet, there is no evidence that they established their political supremacy through military conquest. Maquet, a keen ethnographer of Rwandan affairs, is of the opinion that:

> As the Tutsi migration seems to have been gradual and peaceful, an infiltration rather than a conquest, it is probable that at the beginning their cattle grazed on the unoccupied grasslands. But the population increased as more Tutsi kept on entering the country and more land had to be tilled to feed them. Cattle were also increasing and the Hutu had to move from the most fertile soil, ... This process must have been in operation for a few centuries to produce the situation as we know it now[15].

This is contrary to the usual conquest story. As in Bunyoro, land was plentiful in the areas of migration of the Bahima. To satisfy their grazing needs, they did not, initially, have to encroach on occupied land. Even more important than this is the fact that the original inhabitants in Rwanda did not have a sense of territory in the political meaning but rather of usufruct rights in an unbounded area. Maquet comes closest to it when he states that:

> The Rwanda did not conceive of ownership as a private and exclusive right to the various uses to which a thing may be submitted. They regarded each of the uses as the object of a particular right[16].

Here, Maquet confuses the issue by introducing the concept of "ownership" at all. The concept of "usufruct rights" is probably what the nomads and the agriculturalists had in common and suited both, as long as they were not pressing on each other. This principle might be true of all segmentary societies, as will be argued later: one lineage is as good and as free as another. If at the beginning neither the agriculturalists nor the nomads were unduly worried about the presence of the other, this must have created grounds for a slow and unforced interaction. In this interaction the pastoralists had the monopoly of prestige goods in the form of cattle and of para-military organization. Above all, as immigrants from Bunyoro, they must have had notions about centralization of power. Therefore, if the Bahutu cultivators contributed, materially, to the rise of the state in Rwanda and Ankore, their fate as a subordinate category was already sealed. This is

---

15 Maquet, op. cit., p. 12.
16 Maquet, op. cit., p. 89.

consistent with our general argument that Bunyoro by its early rise provided a model for as well as a challenge to the other peoples in the region.

The Bahima in Ankole, Burundi and Rwanda were not only the descendants of Bahuma in Bunyoro but also their social successors in the historical sense. As Stenning remarks:

> In common with the Nyoro, Toro and some Rwanda, Nyankole trace the descent of their kings from the mythical Chwezi and particularly the king, Ndahura, who ruled the vast kingdom of Kitara. Ndahura's sons were put to govern different parts of the kingdom, and the ruler of what became Ankole was Wamala ...[17].

If at the beginning the Bairu and Bahima were not bound by any common political system but were governed by the heads of their lineages, they could have done so only because Ankore was a province of Bunyoro. Although none of the authorities on Ankore is able to say at what point Ankore became independent of Bunyoro, it is obvious that Ankore could not have asserted its independence against Bunyoro, without a centralized political authority with a creditable military capability. Objectively, the Bahima were the best placed section of the populace to fulfil this role. However, they could not have done so without securing their rear. Their territorial responsibilities necessarily meant hegemonic power from within. Whatever else might be said in mitigation, the Bairu were the objects of such power.

Confirmation of this point comes from several sources. Stenning, while acknowledging the possibility of a symbiotic relationship in the early stages between the Bairu and Bahima, observes that at a certain stage:

> Differential legal and political statuses of Iru and Hima were associated with relationships pertaining to the latter's state organization. With the growth of central organization, the exchange between Hima and Iru became not only that of commodity for commodity, but of goods for services. Iru furnished tribute ... to the Hima state in exchange for military protection by Hima warriors[18].

Similar observations have been made by writers such as Audrey Richards and Beattie[19]. The fact seems to be incontestable. In a more recent study Doornbos expresses himself in a similar vein:

---

17 Richards, op. cit., p. 147.
18 Richards, A., op. cit., p. 153.
19 Richards, A., op. cit., pp. 30-100 and Beattie, op. cit.. p. .....

The division between Bairu and Bahima doubtless constituted the single most important feature of the socio-political structure of Nkore. Put in its briefest form, the division basically rested on three overlapping criteria, differential occupation, status and ethnicity. The Nkore political elite was drawn almost exclusively from the Bahima segment of the population, whereas the Bairu stood largely outside direct political involvements in the state system and in a variety of areas enjoyed lesser rights and privileges in their contacts with the Bahima[20].

What is missing in these statements is an account of the factors behind such developments. Here, are we dealing with politics of conquest or gradual usurpation of power by the Bahima, facilitated by a particular social division of labour? We can only speculate.

The "disappearance" or flight of the Bachwezi from Bunyoro marked drastic changes in their political fortunes. Having left under pressure from another political force, their descendants, the Bahima (if our hypothesis is correct), must have come to guard their independence in the countries of their immigration with jealousy. This is particularly true, if the Bunyoro-Kitara empire was the creation of the Babito who presumably kicked out the forebears of the Bahima. Be it noted that there is no general agreement on this point. Some writers such as Stenning[21] associate Bunyoro-Kitara with the reign of the Bachwezi kings such as Ndahura, while others such as Beattie[22] link it with the advent of the Babito dynasty. However, all are agreed that Bunyoro-Kitara was a vast empire, stretching as far south as Buhaya and Rwanda in the south-west. It is unlikely that rulers who were able to maintain such a vast empire would have been ousted from power without struggle. From Stenning's testimony we hear that as late as the 18th century Bunyoro forces carried out raids as far south as Ankore and Rwanda: In his words:

> The latter (Ntare, king of Ankore) had his revenge when the forces of Bunyoro, returning from a raid in Rwanda, were decimated by Ntare and his warriors. From this event Kaaro-Karung[23] became known as Nkore[24].

---

20   Doombos, M.R., *Not All the King's Men*, The Hague, 1978, p. 27.
21   Richards, A., op. cit., p. 147.
22   Richards, A., op. cit., pp. 100-1.
23   Kaaro-Karungi was part of the vast state founded by one the descendants of Banyoro kings, Ruhinda which became independent after his death (see p. 32).
24   Richards, A. op. cit., p. 155.

From this and other accounts, it is apparent that Bunyoro was trying to assert her authority, but was being challenged by a number of her far-flung tributaries.

It can, therefore, be postulated that the development of the Bahima states in the south was largely a reaction against the hegemony of Bunyoro. This would seem self-evident, despite the fact that some historians such as Karugire are inclined to think that the interlacustrine kingdoms arose as a "defensive mechanism" against the Luo advances from the north. Anthropologically and historically, it is important to note that it was not the Luo who were advancing south. It was rather the Bahuma from Bunyoro, who had not only lost their original language but had also assimilated Bairu culture and "blood", as Beattie is careful to point out. It must be acknowledged that the historical significance of Bunyoro lies in the fact that it initiated the process of centralization of political power in the region through a synthesis of diverse elements. Its empire-building activities meant a progressive dissociation not only between kinship and polity, but also between ethnicity and polity. Different people could and did live under the same political authority in the majority of the interlacustrine states.

Secondly, far from establishing a well-integrated empire, Bunyoro was spawning new kingdoms. As Beattie warns us, despite the general acknowledgement of the suzerainty of Bunyoro over a very wide area,

> It would be a mistake to picture the whole as an orderly and well-administered political unit. There were frequent revolts sometimes led by dissident 'princes', members of the royal Bito clan ...[25].

Thirdly, all historical evidence points to the fact that the crucible from which the Bahima fanned out, once they had entered the interlacustrine region, was Bunyoro. Consequently, the various Bahima dynasties in the region trace their descent to the founding dynasty in Bunyoro. The case for the south-western kingdoms of Ankole, Rwanda and Burundi is more or less settled. Now, it remains for us to turn to the other heterogeneous kingdoms which were not necessarily ruled by Bahima dynasties.

A cursory glance at the south eastern kingdoms of Buhaya, Buzinza and Buha would seem to confirm the argument that Bunyoro was the fountain from which sprang the various interlacustrine kingdoms. In Buhaya the most important ruling dynasty belonged to the Bahinda clan which, according to oral traditions, was an offshoot of the Babito of Bunyoro. It is believed that Ruhinda, the founder of the dynasty, was a son of the king of Bunyoro.

---

25   Beattie, J. op. cit., p. 18.

According to legend, he travelled south along Lake Victoria, conquering as he went. Of relevance to us is the fact that his military escapades were distinct from those of the Bahima, some of whose herdsmen wandered to Buhaya, but did not found any kingdom. Consequently, by the 19th century Buhaya constituted a three-tiered society - the ruling Bahinda dynasty, the Bahima pastoralists plus the Bahinda who did not belong to the royal clan, and the Bairu agriculturalists. Since endogamy was limited only to the Bahinda dynasty, intermarriage was quite permissible among the non-royal Bahinda, Bahima and even Bairu clans, hence Cory's famed classification of the Bahaya clans included "bastardized" clans. This is reminiscent of the admixture found in Bunyoro, and perhaps not so much in Ankore, Burundi and Rwanda. But not dissimilar to the latter kingdoms is the political dominance of the Bahinda clans, descendants of the Babito from Bunyoro who had long lost their original tongue (Luo) and were assimilating into their ranks some Bahima and Bairu clans. Owing to the fact that founding kings appointed their sons as rulers over outlying districts, prospects for rebellion were good. We receive confirmation of this point from La Fontaine and Richards:

> No centralized government for the whole of Buhaya had been achieved at the time of Speke's visit (1861-62) and in fact ... the process of appointing princes to rule over small groups of villages tended to lead to the proliferation of new chiefdoms rather than to their amalgamation. The legends of Buhaya are full of tales of rebellious sons, avenging fathers, and fratricidal strife ending in the splitting of kingdoms[26].

From this observation the authors concluded that: "Buhaya must be reckoned as a multi-kingdom tribe." Probably, at this point in time Buhaya was neither a kingdom nor a tribe, but a society in transition from segmentary to centralized forms of political organization. Here, there are two points to bear in mind. First, while the setting up of petty kingdoms by rebellious princes represented fragmentation of state authority, the reliance of such princes on the support of the local population meant the integration of diverse groups of people into the processes of state-formation over a wide area. The fact that the frontiers of each petty kingdom varied with the fortunes of the day and the political acumen of the incumbent is immaterial. What is of great significance is the fact that a pervasive social formation was evolving in the region, raising prospects for the creation of greater polities. For example, we hear that:

---

26   Richards, A. op. cit., p. 178.

Some of the kingdoms were of considerable size. Karagwe, for instance, the most westerly chiefdom in modern Buhaya,, was evidently comparable to Bunyoro in the scope of its empire and the state its monarch kept at the time of Speke's visit[27].

In fact our hunch is that most of the so-called petty kingdoms of Buhaya were spawned by the Karagwe empire whose history, unlike Bunyoro, has not received the attention it deserves. Nor is that all. The name "Buhaya" itself symbolizes the extension of the name of the original coastal villages on Lake Victoria to cover the whole of Bukoba, as the processes of political integration advanced. Thus, the integration of the original autonomous tribal groups to form a veritable kingdom cannot sensibly be referred to as a super or "multi-kingdom" tribe. It marked a different stage of political development.

From this point of view, it is important to note that the southern neighbour of Buhaya, Buzinza, was associated with Karagwe. Not only is it related, linguistically, to Buhaya, but it was also founded by an off-shoot from the same parent body as the Buhaya kingdoms viz., Karagwe. It is important to get the historical sequence correct here, for once the original Babito from Bunyoro had settled in the area, they became part of the local scene. Indeed, there are some strong parallels between Buzinza and Buhaya. In Buzinza, as in Buhaya, we find the same pattern of social organization. At the top of the pyramid was the Bahinda or members of the royal dynasty, next the Bahuma pastoralists and at the bottom the Bairu cultivators. Ethnographic reports show that in both areas, the Bahinda and the Bahuma were closely identified and that the term "Bahinda" referred only to those who belonged to the ruling dynasty. Otherwise, the rest of the Bahinda were classified as Bahuma. As far as the sub-region is concerned, two parallel processes were in progress. On the one hand, there was consolidation of ruling dynasties over a wide area through lineage and marriage ties and, on the other, a consolidation of a commoner class, irrespective of ethnic origin. As La Fontaine observes, Bahuma and Bairu were not clearly differentiated, as such. There were clans with both Bahuma and Bairu branches and some of the ruling Bahinda dynasties came from such clans. Moreover, the distinction between Bahuma herdsmen and Bairu farmers did not necessarily mean inequality of status.

The processes of integration or assimilation did not end there. Even the ethnographers who were concerned with identifying tribes had to admit that:

---

27   Richards, A., op. cit., p. 177.

It is not possible to speak of Buzinza, the country of the Zinza, in the sense that one can speak of Buganda or Bunyoro. To begin with, there is a large admixture of other tribal groups in all the Zinza chiefdoms. for instance, in Rusubi, which was traditionally a Zinza kingdom, the number of people who describe themselves as Zinza is only 54%, while the rest of the population consists of a mixture of Ha, Nyambo, Rundi and others[28].

Contrary to their own expectations, these ethnographers discovered that: "there is ... a great cultural homogeneity than a mere enumeration of the different elements in the population would suggest ...". It would be remembered that during the 19th century the main slave and trade route from the east coast to Buganda and Bunyoro passed through Buzinza. It, therefore, became a centre of raids, exchange and intermingling of peoples from far and wide. These were no mere tribal phenomena. Even so, none of the competing dynasties had been able to impose its authority over the whole area since the fall of Karagwe. Nonetheless, the processes of political integration in Buzinza were not as advanced as in Buhaya, despite the existence of long-distance trade. This might have had something to do with the class-structure of each society - a point to which we shall return later.

Buzinza's western neighbour, Buha, showed the same general social characteristics. It consisted of a number of petty kingdoms ruled by dynasties which had the same kinship and ethnic affinities. Unlike in Buhaya and Buzinza, where such dynasties were drawn from the Babito immigrants, in Buha they were drawn from the Batutsi (i.e. Bahima) immigrants from Burundi. As in Burundi, Rwanda and Ankore, the Batutsi formed a distinct social category, marked by marriage and eating taboos. But unlike in the other Batutsi/Bahima dominated kingdoms, this did not translate itself into a sharp division between pastoralists and agriculturalists. According to available evidence, both Batutsi and Baha claim a pastoral tradition and both engage in agriculture[29]. But it seems that the Batutsi often relied on the labour of servants and clients. What emerges from this is a two-tiered society, consisting of Baha commoners and a rather diffuse Batutsi upper stratum. Here, the terms "caste" and "aristocracy" are consciously avoided, as the Batutsi dynasties in Buha did not resemble anything like the aristocratic splendour of the Batutsi kings in Burundi, Rwanda and Ankore. It is evident that they were not drawn from the royal

28   Richards, A., op. cit., p. 196.
29   see Richards, A., op. cit., p. 214.

lineages that stayed behind to found great kingship institutions, but rather from the wandering, warlike herdsmen who kept moving eastwards. The units over which they presided could have easily been referred to as chiefdoms rather than kingdoms, awaiting assimilation into the latter as happened in Karagwe.

So far we have followed the development of the kingdoms which were established by the descendants of the founders of Bunyoro, namely, the Bahuma and the Babito who came from outside the interlacustrine region. To avoid any diffusionist presumptions, we emphasized the fact that these people, whoever they were, became assimilated linguistically, culturally and to a great extent socially. Secondly, in the absence of any record of the Galla and Luo pastoralists (or nomadic pastoralists in general) having established kingdoms or a civilization, we attributed the rise of kingdoms in the interlacustrine region possibly to the existence of settled agriculturalists who provided a basis for exchange of goods and services among otherwise diverse groups. In this context Buganda and Busoga should be seen as a test case.

Homogeneous Formations

Although Speke in 1862 was bold enough to tell Mutesa, the king of Buganda, that his people were Galla by origin, and despite the fact that he was able to sell this story to other European travellers, there is hardly any evidence for his claim. First of all, none of the physical characteristics attributed to so-called "Hamitic" ancestory are found among the Baganda and Basoga. Secondly, both Buganda and southern Busoga boast of no pastoral traditions. Consequently, they are free of the division between superordinate pastoralists and subordinate agriculturalists. Both peoples are traditionally agriculturalists, and yet they are not known as "Bairu", as elsewhere in the interlacustrine. Could the term have been introduced by the pastoralists to describe a mode of existence or occupation rather than a genetic stock? The fact that the two coincided cuts no ice.

Anthropologically, it is unlikely that so many communities over such a vast territory and which originally were so isolated from one another could be known by the same name. "Tribal" organization necessitates that each group, even if related to others linguistically and culturally, be known by a specific name. How could the European ethnographers in the interlanstrine region, who accepted unquestioningly the ubiquity of tribes in Africa, have missed this point? Or are we to treat the Baganda and Basoga agriculturalists as exceptions? It seems more sensible to assume that the names of the various interlacustrine kingdoms, like elsewhere in Africa, are synonymous with what the original inhabitants called themselves - Banyoro, Batoro, Banyankole, Bahaya, Bazinza, Baha, Barundi and BanyaRwanda. In the circumstances the term "Bairu" must be regarded as largely a status or occupational reference in the same way as the terms, "Muhuma"/"Muhima/"Muhinda"/"Mututsi" is associated with status or political office in Bunyoro, Buhaya, Buha and Buzinza, irrespective of pedigree.

This makes it possible to account for the rise of Buganda and Busoga, without dissociating either the Baganda or the Basoga from their fellow-agriculturalists in the region. This might seem like swimming against the current, given the strong tradition among ethnographers and natives alike to conjure up outlandish hero-kings as a claim to superiority. Although the Baganda have as their mythical ancestor Kintu (the root of which in Bantu languages means nothing more than human being), they also have their hero-king, Kimera, who hailed from Bunyoro. From this Richards concludes that "... the royal dynasty of Buganda is presumably of "Nilotic" 'Bito' origin, as is the royal family of Bunyoro"[30]. A credulous African historian, without giving any further evidence, merely asserts that the same family that founded Bunyoro founded Buganda[31]. But there are two dynasties which are associated with the rise of Bunyoro - the Bachwezi and Babito. In the absence of any Bachwezi traditions among the Baganda, as is emphasized by Richards[32], it can only be assumed that this refers to the Babito who are supposed to have been as dark-skinned as the Baganda. This would make the Buganda kingdom at least one hundred years younger than Bunyoro, despite the somewhat exaggerated claims of antiquity by Baganda nationalist historians such as Kiwanuka[33].

Even the Babito legend will not do for a number of reasons. First, the Babito were pastoralists and carried with them, wherever they went in the interlacustrine region, pastoral traditions. There is a remarkable absence of such traditions in Buganda. Richards states quite explicitly:

> The ritual of the royal dairy and the sacred herds was not carried out by the Kabaka (king of Buganda) as it was by the kings of Bunyoro, Toro and Ankole; nor were milk, beef and vegetable taboos kept[34].

Secondly, the territory originally occupied by the Baganda fell in the semi-equatorial forest zone interspersed with thick elephant grass which, as

---

30   Op. cit., p. 43.
31   Karugire, S.R., *A Political History of Uganda*, Nairobi, 1980, pp. 7, 21.
32   Op. cit. p. 43.
33   Kiwanuka, M.S.M., *A History of Buganda*, London, 1971, p. iii.
34   Op. cit., p. 44.

any herdsman knows, is not suitable for cattle rearing. Thirdly, Luganda falls outside Lunyoro and the languages of the people among whom the Babito/Bahinda are known to have settled. Fourthly, unlike the Bunyoro dynasties and their off-shoots elsewhere in the interlacustrine region, Buganda had no royal clans; all clans could compete for the throne. Kiwanuka is emphatic on this point:

> ... there was no ruling clan in Buganda and there is no evidence to suggest that such ever existed[35].

In the absence of any substantiable connections between Buganda and the founding dynasties of Bunyoro, we are left with only one possibility, namely, that Buganda was founded by the Baganda - an agricultural people who are indigenous in the area. Kiwanuka claims that by the beginning of the 16th century:

> Buganda was still a disjointed kingdom with many areas still under the effective rule of heads of clans who, however, acknowledged in one form or another the overlordship of the kings of Buganda[36].

He produces no evidence for the latter. And yet, it is crucial to know at what point the kings of Buganda became a sovereign authority, instead of being first among equals in a segmentary society. Kiwanuku traces the origins of the kingdom of Buganda to as far back as the 13th century. But in the same breath he maintains that in the 1200-1400 centuries "Kiganda society was still migratory"[37].

It may be pointed out that not only does the establishment of a kingdom presupposes the existence of a settled society, but also that there is no apparent reason why the Baganda were migratory. Since their agriculture was based on plantains, it must have served them best to remain within the semi-tropical forest zone. furthermore, plantain, as a permanent crop, guaranteed their sedentarisation. This is probably how they were by-passed by the Bahima and Babito pastoralists, as was hinted earlier. In conclusion it must be noted that the importance of Buganda does not reside in its chronological but rather in its social age. In our view Buganda reached the same level of development as Bunyoro in the hands of an indigenous agricultural population which was degraded elsewhere in the interlacustrine region. It is a contrary example whose historical importance cannot be

---

35   Kiwanuka, M.S.M., op. cit., p. 58.
36   Op. cit., p. 41.
37   Op. cit., p. 2.

minimized, given the prevalence of racist and diffusionist theories in the historiography of the region.

Further clarification of the case for Buganda is furnished by its eastern neighbour, Busoga. As in Buganda, there is no trace of the division of the population into dominant pastoralists and servile agriculturalists. Secondly, it is generally acknowledged that there is a definite linguistic affinity between Luganda and Lusoga. However, what is often overlooked in this observation is that, linguistically, there is a marked difference between north-eastern and south-western Busoga. The dialect spoken in the north is Lupakoyo, while the Southerners speak Lutenga. What is of critical importance to us is the way in which this division evolved. First, Lupakoyo is related to the Lunyoro group of languages which are found in those areas where the Babito pastoralists settled. According to Fallers, up to the middle of the 19th century when Speke visited the area, northern Busoga was a tributary of Bunyoro[38]. Not only this, ruling dynasties in at least seven of the north-eastern kingdoms of Busoga belonged to the bushbuck clan whose descent is traced to the Babito of Bunyoro. Furthermore, pastoralism is common in the northern part of Busoga. All this points to a history of occupation in the north by the Babito which is confirmed by the oral traditions which ethnographers such as Fallers were able to collect.

In contrast, the ruling dynasties in the south-western kingdoms were believed to be autochthonous or to have originated from the south-east like the Baganda. Indeed, the Basoga traditionally divide themselves into those who came from Bunyoro and those who came from the south-east or from the islands in Lake Victoria. Three points emerge from this discussion. First, Busoga was not a unitary kingdom. Rather, it consisted of a number of autonomous political units which are reminiscent of the clan or lineage structure in segmentary societies. Second, the common people saw themselves as Basoga, irrespective of the origins of the ruling dynasties and denied absolutely any non-Bantu origins[39]. As this is not necessarily true of all of them, it can only be concluded that, as far as they were concerned, Bantu origins carried no negative connotations. Actually, this represents not only integration of different peoples but also of pastoralism and agriculture according to ecological conditions. Third, Busoga is the one example in the interlacustrine region which shows clearly the simultaneous founding of kingdoms by both indigenous agriculturalists and immigrant pastoralists and the creation of a common culture. If the southern Basoga were able to

38   Richards, A., op. cit., p. 80.
39   Fallers, ibid.

develop centralized political institutions parallel to the Northerners who had some infusions from Bunyoro, why could not the Baganda who, as has been shown, are a kindred people do the same?

To push further the argument concerning spontaneous and simultaneous development, we return to the case of Buganda. At the beginning Buganda might not have been any different from the puny kingdoms of southern Busoga. In fact, it is known from archaeological, historical and ethnographic evidence that the original kingdom of Buganda was confined to the now central counties of Busiro, Kyadondo and Mawokota. At this time in history it could have been a tributary of Bunyoro-Kitara, without being occupied by her pastoral dynasties as its terrain was not suited to cattle-herding. There is no question that during the 16th and the 17th centuries Bunyoro-Kitara was by far the strongest kingdom in the region. Being on the immediate southern frontiers of Bunyoro, Buganda could not have accepted the threat posed by Bunyoro with equanimity. It might be no accident that the Baganda kings of all the ruling dynasties in the region accelerated the process of consolidation of state power. They did this by (i) eliminating traditional ritual leaders (towards the end of the 17th century King Lutebi is supposed to have attacked independent ritual leaders and burnt their shrines to make room for his appointees[40]; (ii) eliminating lineage leaders as centres of authority and replacing them with officially appointed chiefs; (iii) liquidating or excluding from royalty all blood princes on the ascension of the new king; (iv) substituting the principle of brother to brother (or even nephew) succession for the usual primogeniture and by avoiding altogether the idea of a ruling clan through reckoning the descendants of kings from their mother's side - otherwise a perversion of the principle of patrilineal descent among the Baganda; and (v) concentrating all trade in Buganda under the direct control of the king. Bunyoro, with its sprawly empire, governed in the outlying districts by royal princes or vassal kings who were prone to rebellion and by heads of lineages who were interested in maximizing local autonomy, was particularly vulnerable to these innovations. The annexation of Butambala and Gomba by Buganda in the 17th century in violation of Bunyoro's overlordship marked the rise of a competing force whose existence was not attributable to ruling dynasties from Bunyoro. These annexations continued throughout the 18th century, as is shown by, first, the fall of Ssingo and part of Kyaggwe to Buganda and, then, Buddu towards the end of the century. During the latter half of the

---

40   Kiwanuka, M.S.M., op. cit., p. 100.

18th century Buganda emerged as the stronger of the two kingdoms. In the process she had managed to establish a new model of political organization. Hers was a unitary structure, which entailed complete integration of conquered territories and assimilation of their inhabitants as subjects. Consequently, by the 19th century the only distinction that existed among the Baganda was that between the king, his senior chiefs and commoners. The Basoga adopted virtually the same model. It is well to remember that Busoga was, politically, a contested territory between Buganda and Bunyoro. Fallers remarks that:

> Towards the end of the nineteenth century the Soga kingdoms appear to have been rather completely dominated by Buganda and Bunyoro and it seems likely that had the British not intervened they would have been swallowed completely by their giant neighbours[41].

Even so, it is noteworthy that the British in their intervention favoured the Buganda mode of political organization and tried to reproduce it in southern Uganda during their tenure. In actuality this marked the disruption of the pre-existing modes of political organization, but not their demise. Therefore, it is still worth enquiring into the exact nature of the previous mode of political organization.

---

41   Richards, A., op. cit., p. 81.

MODES OF POLITICAL ORGANIZATION IN THE INTERLACUSTRINE KINGDOMS

As was stated earlier, in our view the concept of "social formation" has as its components, the economic instance as well as the instance of power. The two achieve articulation within a recognizable socio-cultural context, as is shown by the ethnography of the interlacustrine societies. Modes of political and economic organization are definitely more concrete than social formations and are capable of variation within the same general context. For instance, the organizational differences between Buganda and Bunyoro-Kitara were not a matter of principle but of adaptive responses, relying more or less on the same model of political organization. Here, we seek to make a distinction between a mode of political reproduction in the abstract sense, for example, centralized kingdoms and mode of political organization in the sense of operational mechanisms, for example, composition of administrative hierarchies in the different kingdoms. Of course, there is the problem of at what point do practical adaptations in their cumulation lead to a qualitative change. Sooner or later in our analysis this is one of the problems with which we will be confronted. But for the time being, we wish to stress the idea of variability of forms in a given socio-historical context so as to avoid the pitfalls of unilineal evolutionism.

In the previous section we attached much significance to the appearance of Kitara as the first subject of the processes of political centralization in the interlacustrine region. We maintained that, through a process of challenge and response, this stimulated other peoples in the region to follow suit. However, it is apparent that they were not merely imitating Bunyoro but were applying its model in an innovative way and according to the exigencies of their circumstances. This resulted in variations within broad uniformities of language and culture which overrode ethnic differences in most cases. Superficially, as the authors of *East African Chiefs* did not fail to notice, these comprised in classical terms one-kingdom "tribes", "multi-kingdom" tribes and unitary kingdoms with a "tribal" caste system. The first category is best exemplified by Buganda, while Busoga, Buhaya, Buzinza and Buha fell into the second category. Ankore, Rwanda and Burundi were supposed to fit unambiguously into the third category. This leaves out Bunyoro and Toro which consisted of single kingdoms, but in which the boundaries between an upper stratum of pastoralists, variously known as Bahuma or Bahima, and a lower stratum of agriculturalists, generally known as Bairu, got so attenuated that these terms were virtually emptied of their original connotations. This applies with even greater force to the "multi-kingdoms" of Buhaya, Buzinza and Buha, where the terms Bahinda, Bahima, Batutsi and Bairu came to denote status differences more than anything else. In our view, this provides a fertile ground for investigating the relationship between status categories and ethnic nomenclature. Such an enquiry could have serious repercussions for the whole system of ethnic classification we are accustomed to in conventional literature.

"MULTI-KINGDOM" FORMATIONS

Any attempt to describe accurately the political systems of the interlacustrine region is encumbered with terminological difficulties. Among these may be mentioned "kingdom", "state", "caste", "tribe", "king", "chief" and "peasant". It is not without significance that the only book in which a comparative study of the interlacustrine polities is undertaken is entitled, *East African Chiefs*, and yet in the text it consistently features kings who reigned over kingdoms, whether big or "tiny". Why not chiefs and chiefdoms, as is usual practice in anthropological literature on the rest of East Africa, in central and southern Africa, with the equally inexplicable exceptions of the Lozi, the Swazi and the Zulu?[1].

The second muddle is epitomized by the concept of "multi-kingdom tribes". It is obvious that here the term, "tribe", is used in a purely cultural sense the delimitation of which is a common language. It will be recalled that the 19th century jurists and social evolutionists used the term to denote a particular stage or form of political organization. In contrast, twentieth century ethnographers tended to use it arbitrarily[2]. This was so much so that Schapera in a rather well-received treatise, *Government and Politics in Tribal Societies* (1956), made it a point to re-assert the classical definition of tribes:

> ... separate 'political communities', each claiming exclusive rights to a given territory and managing its affairs independently of external control[3].

---

1   Although we still have the anomaly of Shaka who founded a kingdom, without being acknowledged as a king himself.
2   See Archie Mafeje, *The Ideology of 'Tribalism'*, JMAS, 1971, pp. 253-61.
3   Schapera, *Government and Politics in Tribal Societies*, London, 1956, p. 203.

This would certainly exclude vassal or tributary states, irrespective of their organization. But for the time being, our interest lies in the distinction between kingdoms and tribes.

In theory, "tribes" refer to particular forms of political organization which are kin-based. The chief is the most senior man of the most senior lineage of the founding clan, whether putative or real. This gives him precedence over other heads of clans or lineages. In a segmentary society he is, therefore, nothing more than *primus inter pares*. But the idea of a royal clan and a ruling lineage implied hierarchy and differential access to prestige goods. In principle this is no different from the privileges enjoyed by elders in a lineage structure. This combined with the redistributive function of kin-based groups compels us to treat tribal communities as pre-class societies, i.e. the existing inequalities among members do not amount to an antagonistic relationship. This position has to be adhered to, despite suggestions by writers such as Meillassoux and his followers that the elders in African societies constitute an exploiting class[4]. The ultimate argument against the latter is the cyclical development of domestic groups[5]: the juniors of today are the elders of tomorrow, and no dead elder can stop this.

Although in the literature dealing with pre-colonial African societies, the terms "tribe" and "kingdom" are used more or less interchangeable, it is apparent that there are qualitative differences between the two formations. First, historically-speaking, kingdoms appear much later than "tribes". In so many ways they represent the assimilation of pre-existing segmentary or tribal societies into a unified whole in which the supreme authority is vested in the hands of a non-kinsman. Implicit in this statement is the supposition that the rise of kingdoms, sociologically and historically, represent the supersession of kin-bound forms of political organization. The abandonment of kinship as a basis for political recruitment signals the rise of an official bureaucracy. The council of elders and the members of the royal lineage in tribal societies do not constitute an official bureaucracy but rather a representation of segmentary or particularistic interests. Therefore, the notion of "multi-kingdom tribes" is an unmitigated contradiction in terms.

But the authors of *East African Chiefs*, who belong to the empiricist tradition of anthropologists, were concerned to describe what they thought

---

4   Meillassoux, C., "Form Reproduction to Reproduction", *Economy, and Society*, Vol. 1, No. (Feb., 1972).

5   See Goody, J. (ed.) *The Developmental Cycle in Domestic Groups*; Cambridge Papers in Social Anthropology, University Press, Cambridge, 1968.

they saw, namely, a number of "tiny kingdoms" among the same peoples. However, conceptually, it is a mistake to equate linguistic groups with forms of political organization, irrespective of the level of development of a society. Any number of solidary descent groups could co-exist within the same cultural and linguistic category. Under these conditions the prospects for the rise of competing tribal units are extremely good. Afterall, we have often heard from anthropologists about the "fissiparous" tendencies in Bantu chiefdoms farther south, where defeated sons of the same chief hive off to form a new chiefdom or, strictly speaking, a new ruling lineage. This kind of proliferation of political units is possible only under the tribal mode of organization and is independent of linguistic affinities. Nor is this peculiar to Africa. In Marx's work there are frequent references to "Germanic tribes" - a linguistic categorisation associated with a plurality of tribes. Therefore, the "multi-kingdoms" of Busoga, Buhaya, Buzinza and Buha must be identified according to their internal structures.

Despite their diversity, the Bahaya, Bazinza, Baha and northern Basoga belong to the Lunyoro-speaking people since their dialects fall into that language group. Besides, they have known historical affinities with the Babito of Bunyoro, as was mentioned earlier. This is not as unusual as it may seem. We have the example of the Xhosa-speakers in South Africa who were divided into about fifteen chiefdoms or tribes and were recognized as such by South African ethnographers who shared a common tradition with their East African brethren. At the cultural and linguistic level this did not stop these ethnographers from acknowledging the existence of certain common traits among these people. In fact, the acknowledgement of common identities went as far as the Zulu - and Swazi-speakers, who together with the Xhosa-speakers, formed a recognizable socio-cultural entity, the Nguni[6]. It would not be an unnecessary contrivance to extend the same principle to corresponding groups in the interlacustrine region, as is clearly intended in this study.

So far we have been concerned to distinguish between cultural and linguistic groups and particular modes of political organisation which might be associated with them. Political modes of organisation can, and do, change while the cultural linguistic context in which they are embedded remains more or less the same. In so far as this is true, the cultural-linguistic context which a number of societies might have in common does not tell us anything about their social age. It is rather the articulation between the mode of

---

6   See N.J. van Warmelo in W.D. Hammond-Tooke (ed.), *The Bantu-speaking Peoples of Southern Africa*, London, 1974; pp. 60-68.

political organization and of economic production which determines the age of a society. For instance, it is a question whether the modes of political organization of the Bahaya, Bazinza, Baha and Basoga were identical. We can do no better than give a short description of the structure of their polities.

As far as we can tell, Buha consisted of chiefdoms in the strict sense. Typically, each chiefdom consisted of a chief, sub-chiefs or district governors and village headmen. The sub-chiefs or governors were usually the chief's agnatic relatives or heads of established clans and lineages, all of whom held hereditary posts. In addition, the chief appointed his favourites to certain posts. These officials did not constitute a bureaucracy as they were merely supplementary to the hereditary chiefs who belonged to particular clans and ruling lineages. For instance, according to Scherer[7], before the advent of the Batutsi, Buha was inhabited "by localized patrilineages under the political authority of lineage heads". Apart from ritual duties, the latter are said to have directed agricultural production and distributed garden lands. They also apportioned land in the irrigated river valleys. When a homestead was abandoned, its garden and banana groves reverted to the common pool *muteko*. This is consistent with lineage organization.

But then we are told that the Batutsi superimposed their political system on the original lineage structure and formed a ruling aristocracy or caste. In this instance the word, "aristocracy", is misleading, for the Batutsi merely substituted their clans for the original Baha ruling clans, while maintaining the same segmentary mode of political organization. La Fontaine reports that some of the Batutsi clans established themselves as "royal dynasties". However, further on she states that:

> There seems to have been a tendency for hereditary kinglets to place either sons or brothers as princes over outlying provinces, which in time became independent[8].

Even though lineage heads are supposed to have lost their authority, it is freely acknowledged by our ethnographers that they "retained their rights to allocate land in their lineage territory and to perform rituals"[9]. Then one wonders what authority could they have lost.

Adjudication in cases of dispute and collection of fines had always been the prerogative of chiefs, sub-chiefs and village headmen. As is customary, the chiefs were the only ones who were entitled to gifts from their subjects.

---

7   Richards, A. op. cit., pp. 213-14).
8   Richards, A., op. cit., p. 215.
9   Op. cit., p. 214.

In this connexion the terms "tax" and "tribute" have been used rather indiscriminately by ethnographers. From the study of other interlacustrine societies it is apparent that regular taxation and extraction of tribute signalled the rise of a non-producing class, a movement away from the redistributive tribal system, and the supplanting of kinship rule by an official bureaucracy.

Finally, taboos on intermarriage notwithstanding, there is no evidence that the Batutsi in general constituted a privileged or exploiting class. They tended their own herds and supplementary crops as much as everybody else. But like members of any royal clan among Bantu-speaking tribes, they enjoyed prestige and were treated with deference which was enhanced by their aloofness. For that matter, the word "caste" gives a greater sense of solidarity and common interests among Batutsi clans than is warranted. What applies to Buha seems to apply equally well to Buzinza, despite the stylized and inflated description of what is supposed to be the typical Buzinza kingdom by La Fontaine[10]. From the accounts of explorers such as Speke and judging from the inability of ethnographers such as J.W. Tyler, who did field work in the area, to give a coherent picture of the political structure of Buzinza, it is apparent that Buzinza consisted of a bewildering multiplicity of political units. This was so much so that when the British arrived in the scene, not only did they amalgamate a number of tiny "kingdoms" into bigger administrative units, but also down-graded the resultant units into "chiefdoms", ruled, not by "kings", but by "chiefs".

Without condoning British colonial meddling, it might be pointed out that they were able to do this only among the so-called "multi-kingdom tribes" in the interlacustrine region. In other words, the prevailing state of affairs among these peoples played into the hands of the British. La Fontaine affirms that:

> Before the advent of the Europeans, Zinza kingdoms were in an almost continuous state of fission and accretion, owing to dynastic wars that generally followed the death of a ruler, to the custom of dividing up the kingdom between the dead ruler's brothers and sons, and to efforts of princes of the blood to set up their own independent kingdoms[11].

Despite the grandiose allusions by ethnographers to "kings", "courtiers" and "retainers", it is obvious that here we are dealing with segmentary, tribal structures based largely on kinship.

---

10   Richards, A., op. cit., pp. 199-201.
11   Richards, A., op. cit., p. 197.

However, it should be noted that this has nothing to do with the composite nature of the populace in these chiefdoms. As in Buha, the population in Buzinza was composed of immigrant pastoralists and indigenous agriculturalists. But in Buzinza the patterns of stratification were more complex. The ruling lineages were largely drawn from the Bahinda clans who owed their origins to the Babito of Bunyoro who were, as we know, pastoralists. Those Bahinda who did not belong to ruling dynasties were referred to as Bahuma, a term which was reserved for the descendants of the Bachwezi who were divine kings. Whatever the origins of these peoples, it is evident that by the time they reached Buzinza these terms had come to denote status differences. The non-chiefly Bahinda fell into a residuary category called "Bahuma" in contradistinction to Bairu, indigenous agriculturalists who were at the bottom of the pile. Nevertheless, some of them made their way up the ladder and attained positions of distinction such as district governorships which were hereditary. In this case the lineages and clans of the incumbents were elevated to the status of "Bahuma". Thus, the term Bahuma designated an admixture of non-ruling Bahinda, the Batutsi herdsmen who migrated from Rwanda and Burundi and elevated Bairu clans. While not rulers themselves, the non-dynastic Bahinda and the Bahuma in general enjoyed social prestige and were treated with respect, as in Buha. This rubbed off on the "Huma-ized" Bairu. All these people in their variety regarded themselves as Banzinza, spoke the same language and shared a common culture. La Fontaine refers to a large tribal admixture in all the "Zinza chiefdoms", but concludes significantly enough that:

> There is, however, a greater cultural homogeneity than a mere enumeration of the different elements in the population would suggest, for members of all the surrounding tribes, except the Nyamwezi and Sukuma, have always been, comparatively speaking, easily absorbed into Zinza society[12].

It is interesting to note that in her account La Fontaine uses the terms "chiefdom" and "kingdom" interchangeably[13]. For our purposes we are still in the sphere of chiefdoms where the principle of partilineages is still preponderant and is not interfered with by occasional appointments of non-kinsmen to administrative posts.

Although Buhaya is included among "multi-kingdom tribes", and although the British reduced all its "petty kingdoms" into a limited number

---

12 Richards, A., op. cit., p. 196.
13 Op. cit., pp. 196-98.

(eight) of chiefdoms, Buhaya has to be approached with some circumspection. True enough, the composition and the ranking of the population in Buhaya resembled that of Buzinza. There were the ruling Bahinda dynasties, while the Bahinda who were not in the direct line of succession to the throne were given a special status, "Nfura", according to Cory. Included in this category were the Bahima clans,

> Who were given a very high social status, but who had little political power as they preferred to remain with their herds away from both the court and the agricultural peasants[14].

In addition, there were Cory's "bastardized" clans i.e. Bairu clans which were elevated to the Nfura status by virtue of their services to the ruler and who in the process got assimilated into the commoner Bahinda and Bahima clans, as in Buzinza. The comparison seems to end there.

Two main features distinguish the petty kingdoms of Buhaya from the chiefdoms of Buzinza and Buha. These are the emergence of a definite ruling dynasty and the institution of a formal bureaucracy which over-shadowed clan and lineage heads. With respect to the rise of the bureaucracy, Richards and La Fontaine have this to say:

> Delegated political power was in the hands of two main categories of authorities - the princes *balangira* drawn from the Hinda dynasty, and the king's own personal followers or clients *batekwa*, that is, his ministers, army leaders, courtiers or messengers[15].

Of particular relevance to us is the fact that the king's appointees were commoners, and yet they were closer to the centre of power than the majority of blood princes who were given only small villages over which to preside. Apparently, the object of these appointments was to provide for the princes while making sure that their access to central authority was limited. This did not apply to the courtiers and district governors who were appointed by the king and were dismissible by him. In other words, the centre of power had shifted significantly towards the sovereign and his appointees.

The second dramatic departure is that in Buhaya, unlike in Buha and Buzinza, the sovereign authority had effective control over land. He had the right to give out estates to his officials. The following extract from Richards is quite explicit:

---

14   Richards, A., op. cit., p. 176.
15   Richards, A., op. cit., p. 180.

Rulers had large estates of their own, on which their tenants lived and gave service; other members of the royal family had like privileges, although their estates were smaller. The rulers gave estates as fiefs *nyarubanja* to faithful followers such as courtiers, administrators and army leaders, and they also gave out land to princes of the blood[16].

The king's control over land does not seem to have been absolute, for Cory reported that some clan estates survived and that clan heads retained their authority over matters of inheritance and succession. But all this was at least in theory subject to the approval of the king, who also reserved the right to create heritable estates. Otherwise, all official estates were used at the discretion of the king. We witness here a basic division of the population into dues - or tribute-paying tenants and privileged overlords who, nonetheless, had no permanent rights in land. Whatever the details, the way was open to private accumulation and the boundary between tribal organization and economy and class society had been crossed.

How did it all happen within the confines of such petty kingdoms which, after all, were on the same scale as the chiefdoms of Buha and Buzinza? Historically, the more advanced processes of centralization of power in Buhaya must be attributed to the existence of the Karagwe empire which was founded by one of the sons of the king of Bunyoro, Ruhinda. Whatever his exact genealogical connections with the kings of Bunyoro, it is apparent that he followed the same model of political organization as in Bunyoro. This would explain the capacity of his kingdom to incorporate other groups and to establish a great empire, covering most of Buhaya, Buzinza and, probably, Buha, according to some sources[17], during the 17th and 18th centuries. One supposition is that what led to the disintegration of Karagwe was lack of strong military organization and the practice of appointing royal princes as governors of districts. As in Bunyoro, these asserted their independence after the death of their father. So by the end of the 19th century Karagwe had disintegrated into a number of small kingdoms which, organisationally, were miniatures of the original kingdom. This is not so dissimilar to what happened in Bunyoro, except that not all her break-away or filial kingdoms were miniature. If so, then we have to explain why the advanced formations in Buhaya and not in Buzinza and Buha. The

16   Op. cit., p. 179.
17   Kimambo, I.N., 'The Interior Before 1800', *A History of Tanzania*, Nairobi, 1969, and Katoke, I., *Karagwe: A Pre-Colonial State*, 1971 and *The Karagwe Kingdom*, Nairobi, 1975.

qualitative differences between the Buhaya and the Buzinza-Buha kingdoms is such that the possibility of a common history among them must be ruled out. The influence of the political model of Karagwe is reflected only in Buhaya, where the segmentary form of political organization prevailed before the advent of Ruhinda. But what caused the decline of Karagwe?

According to Kimambo, who rejects the idea of subjugation of the original inhabitants by conquest,

> It is believed that the Bito dynasty in Bunyoro kept on trying, though in vain, to gain control over the Hinda states. Near the end of the eighteenth century the Banyoro are said to have invaded Karagwe when Ntare VI was ruling. During this period Buha may have been a strong chiefdom since it was with its help that Ntare was able to drive out the invaders[18].

Two points emerge from this account. The first implication is that Buzinza was independent of but allied with Karagwe against Bunyoro. Second, if Karagwe was strong enough to withstand repeated onslaughts from Bunyoro, then absolute lack of military power could not be the explanation for its disintegration in the late 19th century. This would be the case only if the different principalities created by the king himself fielded the fighters when the need arose. This points to the crucial role of a standing army in the process of centralization of political power. Lack of a standing army was probably the reason for the downfall of Karagwe.

Further clues on the impact of Karagwe on the Buhaya kingdoms might be found by examining the case of Busoga - the last example of a "multi-kingdom tribe" in the interlacustrine region. Like Buhaya, Busoga was divided into a number of small kingdoms. As in Buhaya, the political hierarchy of each kingdom consisted of the kinglet at the top, with his subordinates at the district and village level. As in Buhaya, these were comprised of commoner appointees and royal princes. But unlike in Buhaya, both types appeared at either level. As in Buhaya, all officials held fiefdoms in which they collected tribute on their behalf and that of the sovereign. In a like manner those allotted to commoner office-holders were in principle not heritable. Once again, clan heads did not feature much in the political organization of the various kingdoms, except as appointees of the kinglet. It is, therefore, apparent that in Busoga, as in Buhaya, the lineage principle of political organization had been supplanted by the bureaucratic principle and centralized authority in the hands of a king who did not see himself as representing clan or lineage interests.

---

18   Kimambo, op. cit., pp. 21-22.

SINGLE-KINGDOM SOCIAL FORMATIONS

It is worth noting that, historically and sociologically, the principle of kingship is independent of size of social unit. Buhaya and Busoga are a case in point. Nevertheless, it can be presumed, without denying the opposite, that centralizing tendencies imply incorporation of smaller units by bigger or stronger ones over time, especially if they all occupy contiguous territory. This would account for the rise of single kingdoms where several kinglets or tribes once existed. Here, we are not referring to empires but rather to integrated, unitary structures. In the interlacustrine region this has assumed two forms, namely, those kingdoms in which the citizenry was, according to popular notions, divisible into more than one ethnic group and those which consisted of only one ethnic group. Bunyoro, Toro, Ankore, Rwanda and Burundi exemplified the former, while Buganda epitomized the latter. For the sake of convenience, we will start with the so-called multi-ethnic kingdoms, bearing in mind that what is at issue is not ethnic composition but systems of social classification.

"Multi-ethnic" Kingdoms

As we suggested earlier, Bunyoro is a prototype of the interlacustrine kingdoms. Not only did it achieve centralization of political authority at an early date, but also it was its dynasties which inaugurated most of the southern kingdoms. Thus, they created what came to be known as "multi-ethnic" kingdoms. The common view among anthropologists as well as historians is that the rise of Bunyoro itself is attributable to the arrival of some pastoralists from the north. While this must have obviously created an admixture of ethnic groups, there are no compelling grounds for believing that the creation of the Bunyoro state was the work of any particular ethnic group or that ethnic groups persisted throughout its history. The rise of dynasties such as the Bachwezi and the Babito, like the rise of an official bureaucracy, should be seen more as class phenomena than as ethnic epiphenomena. It is significant that the term "Banyoro" originally referred not to people but to political rank, the great territorial chiefs who were accountable only to the king. At this time only two categories of people were recognized, the Bairu agriculturalists and the Bahuma pastoralists, which did not correspond to rulers and the ruled, as is often supposed. Even though the Bahuma pastoralists enjoyed prestige, like everybody else, they were subject to political control by an official bureaucracy. Beattie summarizes the situation as follows:

To the question who could become chiefs in the traditional system, the simplest answer is those whom the Mukama (king) wished to make chiefs. Chieftainships were not restricted to any particular class or category of persons, and Bito (members of the royal clan), Huma and persons of agricultural (though usually of chiefly family) were equally eligible. The usual ground ... for appointment to a chieftainship was that the recipient had either by service or by gift earned the Mukama's approbation[19].

It is apparent that, apart from the royal clan, political office in Bunyoro was independent of ethnic origin. Indeed, since the "disappearance" of the Bachwezi, the kings and princes of Bunyoro were not Bahuma by patrilineal descent but rather Babito by descent as in Buhaya and Buha. Therefore, for all intents and purposes, the Bahuma were commoners whose only distinction was possession of a prestige good i.e. cattle. They were not apart from those Bairu who, in the meantime, had acquired cattle or had been appointed to official posts. In summary, it may be stated that the mode of political organization in Bunyoro was largely bureaucratic. Apart from an hereditary Babito dynasty, the bureaucracy consisted of appointed chiefs who differed in rank. There were the territorial chiefs *bakungu*, the district chiefs *batongole* and the village chiefs. The senior chiefs held great estates in fief directly from the king *Omukama*, but had a good chance of passing them on to their heirs with the permission of the monarch. Lesser chiefs held lesser estates which they derived from territorial chiefs or directly from the king. All the chiefs were entitled to tribute from the tenants in their domains. They also collected taxes from the ruled. These consisted of cattle, dairy and agricultural products. They were also responsible for recruiting labour for public works, military services and for the maintenance of the royal enclosures. Apart from the usual patron-client relationship between chiefs and their chosen subordinates, there was no direct exploitation of the tenants as labour. The extraction of economic value took a political form. Therefore, the question of whether or not there was a ruling class in Bunyoro will have to await further analysis. But in the meantime we note that in Bunyoro the transition from kinship to the bureaucratic mode of political organization had been completed. Secondly, although not yet formalized, property in land had developed to a significant extent through gradual

---

19   Richards, A., op. cit., p. 104.

conversion of official estates into heritable property. Even the idea of extensive official estates in practice meant progressive attenuation of the usufruct rights of the ordinary inhabitants, as was revealed by a government report in 1931[20].

Closely related to Bunyoro by historical origin is Toro (which became Butoro under British rule) founded by a rebellious son of the king of Bunyoro as late as 1830. Although the tendency in the literature is thus to treat Toro as a mirror-image of Bunyoro, this is not altogether justified. There are some very important divergences between the two. First, the conflict between the kinship and the bureaucratic mode of political organization had hardly been resolved in Toro, unlike in Bunyoro. The king was still regarded as the head of totemic clans, which were arranged in a hierarchy not dissimilar from that which obtained in Bunyoro. At the apex was the Babito royal clan, followed by the clan of the reigning queen mother. Next came the Bahima, then the Bairu clans and, finally, disgraced clans of all sorts. Although the clans were widely distributed, they still had recognized leaders who formed a link between the official bureaucracy and the local community. They featured strongly in matters of inheritance, succession and arbitration in cases of dispute and selection of young men to be sent to the king's court. Above all, they were still in competition with the bureaucracy in the allocation of land. Not only were there estates for the king and his chiefs but also clans or lineages at the same time. This is reminiscent of Buganda during a transitional stage in the first half of the 19th century. Nonetheless, the dice was cast in favour of the Omukama (king). Not only could he sanction inheritance of official estates but also could create new ones. This could have been only at the expense of communal forms of land tenure, as happened in Buganda and Bunyoro.

As in Bunyoro, the Toro administrative officials were divided into three categories. First were territorial governors *bamasaza* who had their own courts, messengers and pages. Next came the district chiefs who were known as *batongole*. Last were neighbourhood or village chiefs *bakungu*. As will be seen later, the same terms feature in Buganda although not necessarily to denote the same rank. Yet, the general supposition in contemporary historiography is that there are no direct affinities between Toro and Buganda. Given the fact that we are dealing with recent political boundaries and that, physically, there is no barrier between Butoro and Buganda, it is conceivable that at an earlier date the whole area was inhabited

---

20 *Enquiry into Land Tenure and the Kibanja System in Bunyoro, 1931*, compiled by J.G. Rubie and H.B. Thomas, Entebbe, 1932.

by one and the same people. The distinction between non-Bantu pastoralists and Bantu agriculturalists is a later development whose corollary historiographers are prone to overlook, namely, the processes of assimilation and integration. For instance, it is apparent that once Kitara had arisen as a power in the area, the Batoro, whoever they were originally, got drawn into its ambit and away from the Baganda. In other words, the historical juncture determines which factors will be predominant and which ones will not be. For example, whereas in Bunyoro the bureaucracy was dominated by the Babito and Bahuma, in Toro it was dominated by the Babito. According to B. K. Taylor who did field work in Butoro in 1950-52,

> ... most of the territorial administrators were either Bito or Iru: that is to say they were definitely not Hima[21].

Nor is this surprising. By the time Kaboyo broke away from Bunyoro, the Bahuma dynasties had been usurped by the Babito. However, even in Toro the Bahima enjoyed social prestige as long as they possessed wealth in cattle. Even so, their changing social and political fortunes are vividly reflected in the following concluding remark from the *East African Chiefs*:

> Today, owing to a diminution in cattle numbers, the emigration of many Hima, and inter-marriage with Iru and Bito, the Hima constitute a relatively small class of people who frequently possess neither cattle nor distinctive physique[22].

In contrast to the Bahima in Toro, the Bahima who migrated to Ankore and farther south to Rwanda and Burundi enjoyed hegemonic power over the indigenous agriculturalists known as Bairu or Bahutu. As against the three-tiered social formations found in Bunyoro, Toro, Buhaya and Buha, this gave rise to a two-tiered society whose exact nature has been a source of controversy. Terms such as "caste system", "pastoral" or "feudal" aristocracy have been used to describe it. Yet as far as organizational principles are concerned, the situation is fairly simple. At the time of contact neither the indigenous agriculturalists nor the immigrant Bahima pastoralists had centralized polities. Instead, both had segmentary patrilineages which were free of external control. It cannot be ascertained at what point in time one of these lineages got stronger and began to impose itself on the rest and eventually established a dynasty, namely, the Bahinda dynasty. For such an ascendency to occur, military organization must have been a key factor. This

---

21   Richards, op. cit., p. 135.
22   Op. cit., p. 132.

was readily available among pastoralists. It should not be imagined that the leading lineage constituted itself into a kingship from the start. A close study of the pattern of recruitment would suggest that at first the ascending lineage acted as senior or patron to other lineages. For comparison the nearest thing would be the Alur society[23]. This is of crucial importance for two reasons. First, it did not mean the abandonment of the kinship principle for political organization and, secondly, individual pastoralists attached themselves to the chief or leader for military protection. In this way they and their family herds could be better protected against cattle-raiders. Although it went unheeded in an age of fascination with the Omugabeship, this was in fact J.D. Stenning's original thesis, namely, that:

> Perhaps we should regard the kings of the area as having been originally heads of strong pastoral clans, whose numbers enabled them at one to manage their pastoral affairs and to raid for cattle among neighbouring clans. Their power might have attracted neighbouring pastoralists who found it easier to ally themselves by marriage and tribute than to be despoiled. Suffice to say that the principal relation between Hima and the Mugabe in Ankore was a military one, embodied in the institution of clientship *okutoija*[24].

This goes a long way to explain why the agriculturalists did not feature in the political process of state-formation in Ankore. Unlike a Muhima pastoralist-warrior, a Muiru agriculturalist had no immediate interest in swearing fealty to the king. His rights of cultivation were not in jeopardy. Secondly, when the state had been fully formed, most Bairu did not have the wherewithal to sustain a fealty to the king i.e. cattle and military organization. Besides, the monopoly of the Bahima had been fully established and ideologically sanctified. Does this mean that the state belonged to the Bahima, as is often suggested? The answer to this question must be "no".

First of all, the state, properly understood, does not belong to a people but rather to a class or a socially determined category of rulers. In the circumstances the common people are its objects of control. Once Ruhinda had established his *dominium eminens* over the territory of Ankore, his sovereignty extended over all those who were domiciled in the territory, whether they be Bahima or Bairu. The ensuing inequality in the division of labour between the Bahima and the Bairu does not detract from this general

---

23 See Southhall, A.W., *Alur Society*, Cambridge University Press, Cambridge, 1956.
24 Richards, A., op. cit., p. 152.

principle. To argue that the Bairu were outside a supposedly Bahima state is to deny their contribution to statecraft in Ankore and the exactions they endured in the process. Not only did they pay tribute to the king in the form of agricultural products, but they were also his main artisans who included carvers, tanners, clothiers, musicians and, most of all, blacksmiths who fashioned spears, knives and axes. Besides such practical tasks, they also played an important role in the ideological reproduction of state power as the king's magicians, diviners, herbalists and sorcerers. In the mystical sense these operations did not only secure the personal welfare of the king and his courtiers but also, by implication, that of the kingdom as a whole. They also provided the manpower for the day-to-day maintenance of the king's establishment and that of his notables. This is as good a contribution as any other and a reminder that hero-worshipping is a mark of a dying historiography.

It is our hypothesis that both the Bairu and Bahima pastoralist-warriors undergirded state power in Ankore, without being its embodiment. Then, who controlled the state? It transpires that the government of the kingdom centred on the king, his relatives, his wife's relatives and heads of important clans who acted as the king's power brokers. The chief minister *nganzi* and war-band leaders *bakungu* were the only purely bureaucratic appointments. Military prowess went hand in hand with wealth in cattle, as leading warriors were entitled to a share of the booty. In addition, all officials were entitled to tribute, which consisted of agricultural products from Bairu, cattle and dairy products from Bahima. There was neither public nor private property in land. Usufruct rights prevailed under the lineage system. Direct producers, whether pastoralists or agriculturalists, were autonomous and owed personal services only to their chosen patrons. Thus, it is apparent that in the case of Ankore the boundary between lineage and bureaucratic organization had not been crossed. If so, two questions remain. First, did *Omugabe*, his relatives, selected clan heads and warband leaders, and some rich Bahima family heads constitute an aristocracy? In terms of class, was there any significant difference between ordinary Bahima pastoralists and Bairu agriculturalists?

From the available evidence, what can be said with certainty is that the Ankore social formation was characterized by status differences which were politically and ideologically derived rather than based on direct exploitation of labour and property-relations. However, such status differences notwithstanding, both Bahima and Bairu subjects suffered extraction of surplus value in the form of tribute by the rulers. While formally-speaking this referred to the *Omugabe*, his relatives and a few privileged appointees, there was a wider and supplementary stratum of rich cattle-owners who stood in a patron-client relation to the majority of the producers. Along with the royalty and its entourage, these can, without ethnic prejudice, be referred to as a pastoral aristocracy. But, be it noted that, nevertheless, their privileges were not accompanied by ownership of land or its distribution to the direct producers. Tenure and utilization of land was still very much in the hands of heads of lineages.

If Ankore represents a somewhat unresolved interplay between kingship and lineage organization, Burundi farther south exhibited an even greater irresolution of the problem. But this is to be understood in the context of ceaseless efforts by Burundi kings to established a more centralized system of authority. According to oral traditions, Burundi was founded by King Ntare from Buha, which would suggest that he was a Muhinda rather than a Muhima, as is generally the case in the south-western kingdoms. Here two factors intervene which make us doubt the veracity of these oral traditions. First, Ntare is the name of the founding hero of Ankore as well. Secondly, there is evidence to show that the kings of Rwanda and Burundi had a common origin. The founder of the ruling dynasty in Rwanda was Mututsi, allegedly the fourth son of the original hero who descended from heaven. Whatever the exigencies of the story, this gives us the derivation of Batutsi, who in Burundi are concentrated in a region called "Bututsi", as is testified by Lemarchand:

> In Burundi, the bulk of Tutsi elements are found, logically enough, in the Bututsi region, where they make up between 80 and 85 per cent of the local population[25].

The various ruling dynasties in Burundi originated from the same region.

Although there is evidence that the kingdom of Burundi grew by the sword, especially in the first half of the 19th century during the reign of King Rugaamba (c. 1795-1852), it is important to note that this did not amount to politics of conquest as is often supposed. The expansion was accounted for by competition from within. It is apparent that at first, as in Ankore, the country was occupied by autonomous pastoral as well as agricultural patrilineages. Some of these were organized into chiefdoms. Unlike in Ankore, in Burundi chieftaincy was not a monopoly of the descendants of the Bahima, the Batutsi. Not only did the Bahutu chiefs succeed in retaining power in their original territories but also, by virtue of this, they became

---

25   Lemarchand, Rwanda and Burundi, 1970, p. 25.

eligible for bureaucratic posts. Emphasizing the fact, Lemarchand has this to say:

> Indeed, a remarkable feature of the traditional system was the comparatively high proportion of Hutu chiefs who held office in the royal domains (the so-called *ivyivare*)[26].

This is attributable partly to demographic factors, namely that some areas were free of Batutsi inhabitants. But it was due mainly to the mode of political organization in Burundi. As was mentioned earlier, in Burundi the struggle between the monarchy and representatives of solidary kinship groups had not yet been resolved. Secondly, in Burundi the general principle was to extend executive authority to all princes of the blood *baganwa*. This gave rise not only to incessant rivalries among the princes but also to the diminution of central authority. The king, far from being a sovereign power, stayed as first among equals. On this point Lemarchand makes the following observation:

> In Burundi ... where the military structure was conspicuously weak, the contest between the monarchy and corporate descent groups resulted in far greater political decentralization. There was no parallel in Burundi for the centralized, hierarchical pattern of authority found in Rwanda. Instead, power was fragmented among relatively autonomous political units, each under the authority of a prince[27].

It is true that during the period of military expansion in the 19th century the tendency was for the king of Burundi to appoint his sons as governors of newly acquired territories, something which encouraged rebellion among the princes and thus spawned numerous principalities. Even so, this does not take into account the demographic balance in the country. It is unlikely that the princes of the blood were numerous or powerful enough to take charge of all the provinces..

According to early travellers, there were several estates which "were administered by some Bahutu who were not subject to the *baganwa* but acted like independent chiefs". Although Lemarchand treats "chiefs" and "princes" as administrative equivalents, it is obvious that here we are dealing with the transition from chiefdoms to royal dynasties. That is why, in his own words,

---

26 Lemarchand, op. cit., p. 28.
27 Lemarchand, op. cit., p. 22.

Burundi tended to look at best like a loose aggregate of semi-autonomous chiefdoms; at worst like a cluster of warring principalities.

This had to be so because territorial chiefs or royal princes were free to appoint their own sub-chiefs, to raise their own armies in times of war, to exact tribute and administer justice in cases of dispute. Whereas in the literature there is reference to "estates", there is no evidence that the king or the princes in Burundi had arrogated to themselves the right to distribute land. It seems that the term "estate" referred to an administrative domain rather than to official or private property in land. Like in Ankore, access to land appears to have been contingent on kinship affiliations. One could surmise that this was true of royalty as well, for

> The strength of a prince's claims ultimately depended on the genealogical remoteness or proximity of the dynasty from which he claimed descent[28].

By tradition, Burundi, unlike Ankore or Rwanda where only one dynasty reigned, was ruled by four dynasties, Ntare, Mwezi, Mutaga and Mwambutsa. These might have been the sons of the same king, in which case there would have been an acknowledged ranking order among them. But the fact of matter is that their descendants had been vying for ascendancy since the early 19th century. Hence, the tendency was for the state to be fragmented into kinglets who nonetheless never ceased to strive for supreme authority over the whole territory. As the Batutsi were thin on the ground and in the absence of a standing state army, all contenders to power had willy-nilly to rely on a certain amount of support from the Bahutu chiefs and their followers. Indeed, there is evidence that the monarch was only able to hold some balance of power between himself and other pretenders to the throne by enlisting the support of loyal Bahutu leaders. This explains their strong representation in the official bureaucracy. Likewise, warring princes could not hope for a lasting victory, without the support of the local Bahutu population. Therefore, there can be no doubt that in the case of Burundi the agriculturalists were involved in state politics almost at every level. However, this does not say whether or not Burundi was a "multi-ethnic" kingdom. What did the terms "Bahutu" and "Batutsi" denote?

In contrast to the term "Bairu", which we argued was essentially a *status category*, ethnographic detail would indicate that "Bahutu" is a specific term which referred to the indigenous inhabitants of what is now known as

---

28   Lemarchand, op. cit., p. 22.

Rwanda and Burundi. According to available historical evidence, these people were organized into chiefdoms and patrilineages by the time the Bahima pastoralists appeared on the scene during the 16th and 17th centuries. As has been shown already, in Burundi, unlike in Ankore and Rwanda, in subsequent developments the Bahutu did not suffer political degradation as a group. Instead, they became part of a complex pattern of superordination and subordination of members of particular patrilineages. Unlike in the other kingdoms we have encountered so far, in Burundi there was no recognizable ranking of clans according to their origin, except for the royal dynasties mentioned earlier. The latter were derived exclusively from Batutsi clans. Although in the literature the Batutsi are presented as an ethnic group, this is contrary to historical evidence. The pastoralists who migrated to Rwanda and Burundi were Bahima by origin. The interesting question, ethnographically and historically, is at what point did they become Batutsi? If the Batutsi were in fact the descendants of Mututsi, then what became of the rest of the Bahima?

Here, we find a clear example of how tribes are derived independently of "ethnic" origin. In Burundi the Batutsi, as was indicated earlier, got divided into sub-tribes - the Batare, Bezi, Bataga and Bambutsa - whose individual identity took precedence over ethnic origin. Thus, the population of Burundi consisted of royal and non-royal Batutsi, Bahima and Bahutu. Only royal Batutsi enjoyed eminence and power by tradition and by virtue of their descent. The rest were commoners who had to prove themselves in order to be appointed to positions of power. One gets the gist of what we are hinting at from the following extract:

> By far the most important concerns the very prominent status achieved by the princes of the blood, or *Ganwa*, in the political system of Burundi. Because of the special eminence conferred upon them by the accident of history, they became identified as a separate ethnic group, whose prestige in society ranked far above that of the ordinary Tutsi. If, in addition, one remembers that there are in Burundi two disjunctive categories of Tutsi - the 'low-caste' Tutsi-Hima and the 'upper-caste' Tutsi-Banyaruguru - the total picture of society appears decidedly more variegated than in Rwanda[29].

As so often happens, here Lemarchand exhibits the usual indifference to the use of terms such as "ethnic group" and "caste". The Batutsi royal princes could not have constituted an ethnic group by themselves. Secondly, while

---

29   Lemarchand, op. cit., pp. 23-24.

Banyaruguru, which means "people from above", undoubtedly denotes a status distinction, it could not have referred to "caste" since the same reference term was used for equivalent groups among the Bahutu and Bahima. Acknowledgement of the same point comes from Lemarchand himself: "Very much the same type of classification and terminology applies to the Hutu"[30]. Finally, despite the fact that Lemarchand refers to an ethnic category called "Tutsi-Hima", it is apparent that in Burundi the Batutsi had developed a separate identity from the original Bahima. Once again, we get confirmation of this point from Lemarchand when he declares:

> Most other areas have only a sprinkling of Tutsi. About one-third of the country is inhabited by a mixture of Hutu and Hima populations, *with virtually no Tutsi*[31].

Even more important for our purposes is the fact that in Burundi ethnic distinctions became largely irrelevant as a justification for status. Generally-speaking, rank was obtained on other grounds. The following remark by Lemarchand is most pertinent:

> This greater variety of status groups, ranging from prince to commoner, is one major reason why in the past Burundi society was relatively free of racial tensions; just as the degrees of social distance within the Tutsi stratum were at times far more perceptible than between Tutsi and Hutu, the distance between them and the princely families was equally if not more conspicuous[32].

What is difficult to determine is whether the observable social differentiation among the Barundi, cutting across ethnic categories, did in and by itself signify the emergence of a class society. The king and his officers as well as the princes and their entourage received tribute and dues from the direct producers, the pastoralists and the agriculturalists. But neither the king nor the princes held property in land. Claim to land resources was politically determined i.e. administrative domains were the general rule. In the case of autonomous local chiefs as in the case of ordinary citizens the patrilineage was the point of reference. The political strength of the patrilineages and the endemic competition among the princes of the blood set a very severe limit to the amount of exactions office-holders could impose on the population within their domains. The fragmentation of

---

30   Op. cit., fn. p. 24.
31   Op. cit., p. 25 emphasis added.
32   Lemarchand, op. cit., p. 24.

political authority in Burundi also tended to minimize the importance of the usual patron-client relationship. Individuals had ample opportunities for shifting their allegiance. Consequently, in certain areas the vast majority of the Hutu population lived in small, self-contained communities that were virtually immune to contractual obligations.

> If clientship served any purpose at all for the Hutu it was primarily as an avenue for social mobility, rather than as an instrument of Tutsi domination, concludes Lemarchand[33].

Despite the fact that neither property- nor labour-relations could justify the division of Burundi society into classes, it is undeniable that the term *banyaruguru* referred to a definite, privileged stratum in society, consisting of royalty, the princes and an incipient bureaucracy of chiefs and sub-chiefs. All these lived, partially or wholly, on revenues extracted from the general populace. However, they were not as yet independent of their patrilineages.

Closely related to but different from Burundi is Rwanda. There is every reason to suppose that the kings who founded Burundi migrated from Rwanda and were in fact among the descendants of Mututsi. Likewise, the Bahutu on both sides of the border are one and the same people. An interesting ethnographic detail is the disappearance of "Bahima" as an ethnic category in Rwanda. None of the studies on Rwanda makes reference to Bahima as a constituent element of the population of Rwanda. Yet, it is known that the Bahima pastoralists migrated from Bunyoro in a south-westerly direction to Ankore, Rwanda and Burundi. If ethnic categories mean anything at all, it is in Rwanda and not in Burundi where we should find Bahima. Rwanda's physical proximity to Ankore and the fact that, historically, it is prior would predicate so. This adds extra strength to our general argument about the metaphorical nature of ethnic categories. The Batutsi, the descendants of Mututsi, who enjoyed political hegemony in Rwanda over a period of nearly four hundred years and provided virtually all its ruling dynasties or the *abanyiginya* clan eclipsed the Bahima as a status category. From then henceforth the population of Rwanda was divisible into Batutsi, Bahutu and Batwa.

Unlike Burundi, Rwanda had a highly centralized political structure. At the top of the hierarchy was the king *mwami*, who was considered by all counts to be divine i.e. he was supposed to have hailed from heaven and his body was endowed with sanctity. As in Ankore, his mother, the queen-mother *(umugabekazi* = female umugabe), was the second most

---

33   Lemarchand, op. cit., p. 40.

important personage within the royal court. She was the supreme counsellor to the king. In addition, the king had an official council of chiefs who played an advisory role. His most favourite councillor played the role of Prime Minister. All chiefs were appointed by the king and were dismissible by him. They consisted of district and hill chiefs who fell into two categories, land- and cattle-chiefs. As would be expected, the land-chiefs were Bahutu who dealt exclusively with the tillers of the soil. The cattle-chiefs were Batutsi and dealt with the pastoralists. The main function of the chiefs was to collect tribute and dues from the population in their respective domains. These took the form of dairy products and cattle from the pastoralists and agricultural products from the cultivators, especially banana for making beer which had a particular appeal to the Batutsi over-lords. It is worth noting that dues and tribute were demanded not from individuals but from lineage or family heads. Maquet remarks that:

> This way of reaching the individual through his kin group and family group enhanced the importance of the descent principle of kin solidarity[34]

- a point to which we shall return presently. The second important function of the chiefs was to settle disputes over land and cattle. However, whereas the land-chief arbitrated in land cases, the cattle-chief did not judge in cattle disputes. It was rather the army chief who dealt with cattle disputes. The main reason for this is that it was the army which was responsible for raiding for cattle in the neighbouring communities and for protecting national herds.

In contrast to Burundi and most of the interlacustrine kingdoms, Rwanda had a standing army. According to Maquet,

> Every Rwanda, Twa, Hutu as well as a Tutsi, was affiliated to an army. However, recruitment was not on the basis of individuals but of patrilineages. Commenting on the same, Maquet observes: These people were not incorporated individually but with the patrilineage[35].

This emphasizes the juxtaposition between the lineage and the bureaucratic principle in the mode of political organization in Rwanda, despite its apparent high degree of centralization of political power. Maquet is acutely aware of this and concedes that:

---

34   Maquet, J. op. cit., p. 107.
35   Op. cit., p. 110.

Individually, in the difficult or dangerous events of life, a Hutu could rely upon the protection of his lord, of his army-chief, and of his administrative chiefs if he could not or did not wish to ask his lineage's aid[36].

For this reason, Maquet finds no contradiction between the kinship and the territorial basis for political and military organization in Rwanda. Nevertheless, he almost contradicts himself when he declares:

The different functions of the military structure of Rwanda were profitable mainly to the rulers: they contributed to the maintenance in power positions of those who were occupying them. Through that structure, the king secured ... an important amount of commodities ... more cattle ... and a more complete control of all the chiefs under him[37].

In contrast, the only privilege warriors enjoyed was to loot privately after the army had finished its raid. Secondly, while affiliation to the army by all would suggest lack of discrimination and greater political integration than in Ankore, it transpires that only the Batutsi were warriors. The Bahutu and Batwa were restricted to the role of herdsmen who rounded up cattle during a raid or carried supplies for the warriors. As the booty was shared between the political leaders and the army-chiefs, only warriors could have hoped to receive any cattle at all. It is, therefore, obvious that although all citizens were subject to extraction of tribute and dues, there was, as in Ankore, a conscious effort to deny non-Batutsi access to cattle in general. As Maquet points out, cattle were a symbol of prestige and an instrument of power, whose unrestricted distribution would have undermined the position of the Batutsi ruling elite for:

A Tutsi who did not own any cattle was still a Tutsi but a very poor one, dangerously slipping down in the social stratification, whereas a Hutu who possessed cattle was very near the aristocratic group and not infrequently could marry a Tutsi girl[38].

Despite the use of ethnic categories and terms such as "caste" in the literature, even in the case of Rwanda this would indicate processes of class differentiation. What is hard, though, is to characterize them unambiguously.

---

36   Op. cit., p. 158-9.
37   Op. cit., p. 123.
38   Maquet, J. op. cit., p. 120.

In Rwanda, as in the other pastoral kingdoms in the region, there was no property in land but rather political control over it. The king enjoyed *dominium eminens* over the whole country, although this did not necessarily stop some Bahutu chiefs from looking upon themselves as important representatives of local lineages. Nevertheless, the king reserved the right to allocate official estates to his appointed chiefs who had the right to collect tribute and dues from the people over whom they presided. While the land-chiefs acted as judges in land disputes, there is no evidence that they also allocated land to the cultivators. It seems that the role was largely left to heads of patrilineages. However, heads of patrilineages or families more often than not were clients of chiefs or of the king himself. While these patrons could not possibly be described as landlords, they must have exercised appreciable political influence in the allocation of resources, be they arable or grazing land. Secondly, their entitlements to labour-services of up to two days a week from their clients signified some control over the labour process. But in so far as the patron-client relationship was emphasized and in so far as holders of benefices were subject to dismissal, the clients were exploited less as labour than as subjects. This is particularly true of the Batutsi pastoralists who were not liable to labour-dues.

Therefore, we are faced with a situation where there was general exploitation which had not been crystallized into definite labour-relations. Secondly, the exploitative ruling elite, excepting the royal dynasty, had not yet found mechanisms for reproducing itself indefinitely as a class. Since cattle were more important than land in Rwanda and since they were an object of individual appropriation and accumulation, rich cattle-owners could reproduce themselves indefinitely. Moreover, by virtue of their cattle wealth, they were eligible for high office and/or other social privileges. One has *prima facie* a good case for calling such a stratum a pastoral aristocracy, as against a "Batutsi aristocracy" or "caste", since the majority of the Batutsi were neither rich nor exempt from exploitation by the state and its bureaucracy. But was what we are alluding to maximization of utility value or something else? Answers to this question are subject to a more detailed discussion of the mode(s) of production in all the interlacustrine kingdoms.

"Single-ethnic" Kingdoms

Only Buganda falls into this category in the interlacustrine region. By its nature, Buganda might help to throw into relief some of the issues raised above. Like Rwanda, Buganda was highly centralized. But unlike Rwanda and the rest of the unitary kingdoms described above, Buganda was inhabited by one people, the Baganda (a term, oruganda, which, interestingly enough, means "clans" in Rutoro). It was an agricultural society *par excellence* and boasted of no pastoral traditions. Therefore, land was the most important asset on which its rulers could lay claim. As in the other kingdoms, initially the king of Buganda *Kabaka* was first among equal heads of patrilineages or clans *bataka*. However, by the middle of the 19th century, the king had usurped clan heads and had declared himself *Saabataka* (head of all clan heads). This was not in vain because thereafter the king dispensed with the *bataka* as custodians of clan or lineage lands and arrogated the right to distribute land solely unto himself. This is unprecedented in black Africa, barring the Sudan and Ethiopia. It is certainly unique in the interlacustrine region. Having taken control of all land in Buganda, the king was in a position to administer it the way he liked. He did this by appointing his own chiefs who were known as *bakungu*. These were great territorial chiefs comparable to the ones found in Bunyoro and who were also known by the same term. As in Bunyoro, these chiefs were granted big official estates. But unlike in Bunyoro, none of them was able to hold his fiefdom in perpetuity until the British intervention. All territorial chiefs appointed their own assistant chiefs or bailiffs *batongole* with the approval of the *Kabaka*. They acted as sub-district chiefs and were responsible for collecting tribute and dues *busulu* and *nvujjo* from the people who resided in their administrative domains. This was passed on to the senior chiefs *bamasaza* who retained about one-third of what was collected and sent the rest to the king. In addition, there were village chiefs who acted as local policemen and reported to the district chiefs.

The evolving political structure had far-reaching implications. Not only did it mean that the ordinary citizens were closely supervised but that their rights to land outside the official bureaucracy were fore-closed. They had to look up to the chiefs as patrons who could grant or refuse them land for cultivation. But as there was more competition for followers than for land, it was relatively easy for individual Baganda to gain access to land as long as they paid allegiance to a particular chief. This made clients of all ordinary citizens. Conversely, all chiefs were potential patrons who, nonetheless, owed their position to the ultimate patron, the *Kabaka*, by whom they were dismissible. In the event of dismissal, they lost everything and reverted to the status of ordinary people who were variously referred to as *bakopi* (peasants), *basenze* (tenants) or *basajja bangu* (my men). This categorisation was carried to its ultimate conclusion. Not only did fallen chiefs become ordinary "peasants" but also non-blood princes were referred to as "peasant princes", meaning that though they may enjoy prestige and certain privileges they were no longer part of royalty. Here, once again, the Buganda kings, amongst all Bantu-speaking rulers, achieved distinction by violating the principle of unilineal descent. Whereas everybody in patrilineal Buganda belonged to his patrilineage, the centralizing king(s) insisted that monarchs be affiliated to their mother's lineage. The stated rationale for this was "to prevent any single clan from becoming too powerful". In other words, the founding kings of Buganda wished to avoid the development of entrenched dynasties. Consequently, at the ascension of the new king to the throne all blood princes were eliminated. In practice this meant that all clans were eligible for kingship, depending on the mother of the crown-prince. There is no question about it: Buganda among all the known kingdoms amongst Bantu-speakers had gone farthest in abrogating the principle of kinship as a basis for political organization.

Nevertheless, Buganda conspicuously failed to produce the antithesis of communal rights in land i.e. private property in land until the advent of the British. The official bureaucracy was limited to strictly non-heritable estates. In the absence of any other heritable assets such as cattle, the bureaucratically appointed chiefs had no way of reproducing themselves once they had left office. Even the kings who did not constitute a dynasty had poor opportunities for accumulating property through a particular descent line. This was made worse by the fact that all tribute was in the form of perishable goods such as green bananas, beer, fish and bark-cloth. Beyond this, the so-called "clients" or "peasants" were not obliged to render personal services to their patrons. The most they were expected to do was to perform public services such as participations in military expeditions, construction of public roads and maintenance of the enclosures of senior chiefs and the king. Otherwise they had the right of removal *kusenguka*. This implies that, as elsewhere in the interlacustrine, they were exploited not so much as labour but more as loyal subjects or clients. While they referred to all chiefs as *mwami* (my lord), this did not denote "generalized servitude", as was known in the Orient. Rather it symbolized highly personalized dyadic relationships which overlaid latent class antagonism. The fact that enterprising ordinary citizens could be appointed to high positions and disgraced chiefs could be turned in an instance into ordinary *bakopi* made crystallization of classes even more remote. Therefore, if Buganda was advanced in its mode of political organization, it does not follow that it was equally advanced in its organization of the labour process and the realization of property-relations. It may, thus, be asked whether the chiefs of Buganda, untrammelled by any kinship obligations, were on the verge of consolidating themselves into a class in a way which transcended the limitations of pastoralism in a kingdom such as Rwanda. It would appear that accumulation of land in private hands in agricultural societies has different implications from accumulation of cattle by individuals or families in pastoral societies because of the labour process itself and the possibilities for conversion of value.

THE SOCIAL AND ECONOMIC CHARACTER OF THE INTERLA- CUSTRINE KINGDOMS

Both historical and contemporary studies of modes of social production in Africa are handicapped by lack of the necessary data. The main reason is that most of the studies carried out in the region had been partial either because of the division of labour among the various disciplines or because of certain ideological blinkers. Pertaining to the latter, it may be recalled that the concept of "modes of production" is Marxian and Marxists are new-comers in Africa. Liberal scholars, who have been longest in the continent, did not believe in a political economy approach but preferred rather to study aspects of given phenomena (micro-studies). This was especially true of the economists who were happy to study production processes, without bothering much about the social and the political institutions in which these were embedded. This would include even such important institutions as land tenure which was simply stereo-typed as "communal" and regarded as a barrier to development. Likewise, colonial administrators and agriculturalists looked upon African land tenure systems with jaundiced eyes and with the intention of supplanting them with their own and for their own purposes. Thus, the dynamics of African tenure systems and land uses were relegated to the background.

The few African historians there were devoted their attention to human migrations, development of states and empires, and long-distance trade. Land tenure systems and domestic systems of production and exchange hardly interested them. Notable exceptions were anthropologists and some lawyers such as C.K. Meek and A. Allot. However, they too suffered from a formalistic approach to land tenure. Not surprisingly, the result was an idealized charter of land rights, divorced from the dynamics of use and their economic implications. Whenever anthropologists broached the question, they often couched it in kinship terms which was in so many ways a reproduction of local ideologies. Singularly lacking in all the various studies was systematic data on the social and technical conditions for material production in traditional societies - something which was so crucial in the understanding of agrarian societies and their transformations in Europe. This was left largely at the level of circulation of goods. For example, it was often reported that the Bairu agriculturalists and Bahima/Batutsi pastoralists exchanged goods. But we also know that in some instances within the same kingdoms Bairu and Bahima/Batutsi/Bahinda practised both agriculture and pastoralism, without exploiting one another's labour or relying on the patronage of specific overlords *bami*. Did this represent the emergence of the petty commodity mode of production and changing social and technical conditions for production and reproduction? Or was it a reassertion of familial (minimal lineage) forms of economic production under conditions where the dominant mode of social organization could not sustain itself? Or was it simply an articulation of different modes of production under conditions of uneven development? These questions can only be answered by detailed historical studies, using colonial district reports and oral traditions.

The interlacustrine kingdoms have been described by anthropologists, political scientists and historians as "feudal" largely on the account of their super-structural features-kingship, bureaucracy and fiefdoms or clientage. As has been pointed out by Goody in his refreshingly critical study, *Technology, Tradition and the State in Africa*[1], any degree of political centralization entails withdrawal of some manpower from primary production into administrative activities and extraction of some economic value by the political hierarchy. But this is not sufficient. Certain specific features such as dependent tenure, the seigniorial mode of estate management and fiscal arrangements have to be examined before any decision is made as to whether or not what we are dealing with is feudalism. This is what Goody calls the economic approach to feudalism, as against the political or supra-structural approach mentioned above. However, as has been warned in the previous chapter, a separation between the two could be just as undialectical.

Our concern in this chapter is to identify as closely as possible the various modes of production in the interlacustrine kingdoms in terms of production relations and access to means of production rather than in terms of modes of political organization which are easy to generalize, for example,. kingdoms. In any study of agrarian societies land and its uses is the key. But concepts regarding land tenure in Africa are overlaiden with European notions which led to certain misconceptions. These need to be challenged by bringing out the specificity of African social systems, not out of sheer chauvinism but rather with the intention of discerning more clearly the logic of African development or lack of it.

---

1   Goody, J., *Technology, Tradition and the State in Africa*, London, 1971.

African societies are predominantly agrarian and, accordingly, their foundations are in land and its uses. "Land tenure" is the term that has been used to refer to this complex. In Western jurisprudence land tenure is strongly associated with notions of property or ownership, whether individual or corporate. Consequently, in the absence of individual land tenure most Europeans who worked in Africa simply concluded that what they saw was "communal" land tenure. In other words, they did not give up the notion of property but merely acknowledged the fact that it was corporate. As Post has argued in his seminal paper, "Peasantization in Western Africa"[2], it seems that in the case of sub-Saharan Africa land use rights are more important than property rights. From further research and reflection, it would appear that even Post's formulation does not go far enough. The most appropriate thing would be to deny altogether the notion of property in land in pre-colonial Africa and to contemplate the theoretical and practical implications of the primacy of use rights. Conventionally, we are used to thinking that rules or tenure determine use and not the other way round. From a dialectical materialist point of view, it is evident that it is use which gives value to any natural object and that it is in the nature of society to formulate rules to regulate use of resources or social appropriation of nature. Therefore, tenure might not matter, depending on the state of the relationship between man and nature. Hunters and gatherers, who treat nature as a subject of labour, barely have any social need for tenure.

The rise of kingdoms mark a fairly advanced stage in the regulation of resources, including human resources. The interlacustrine kingdoms were at different stages in this process. In Buganda the Kabakas had dispensed with clan heads *bataka* as local custodians over land and had established an absolute monopoly over the distribution of land. As the Kiganda proverb goes, the Kabaka "had eaten up the country". This was universal within the kingdom. The land tenure system consisted of royal and official estates granted to the Kabaka's appointed chiefs and their subordinates. The ordinary citizens could only gain access to the land through supplication to chiefs *kusenga*. This made tenants of them, but not necessarily labouring ones. They were tenants-at-will and had the right of removal *kusenguka*. Secondly, production relations between the chiefs and their tenants *did not* amount to a relationship between a lord and his serfs. The only services the tenants was obliged to render to the chief were public ones, for example,. military services, public works such as building roads and bridges and

---

2   Post, *Peasantization in Western Africa*, 1972.

repairs to the chief's houses and enclosures. Otherwise, for everyday consumption the chief relied on the labour of his wives, concubines, pages and slaves captured in military raids against neighbouring states. The only recognizable form of extraction of economic value from the Baganda tenants *basenze* was dues and tribute *busulu* and *nvujjo*. Both were aimed at raising state revenues and underwrote a higher standard of living, quantitatively, among the chiefs. However, it is worth noting that tribute underlined a political relationship between patrons and clients. The Kabaka was a patron to his chiefs and his chiefs were patrons to their bailiffs and tenants. Without detracting from the general principle, what is of great theoretical significance is the fact that the goods which passed through these hierarchies of dependence were perishable-banana beer *mwenge*, barkcloth, meat, fish or plantains. Under these circumstances the prospects for accumulation at the top were nil. This combined with the fact that the chiefs' estates or administrative domains were *not heritable* and reverted to the Kabaka on the death or dismissal of each chief makes it very difficult to talk of a ruling aristocracy or class in Buganda with reference to property relations. Nor can we speak of a ruling elite on the basis of recruitment. In the same way that chiefs who had fallen out of grace reverted to the status of peasant *mukopi*, likewise politically successful peasants got elevated to chiefly positions. The implications of all these deviations from the classical model are so momentous that they cannot be resolved on the basis of isolated cases. This would emphasize the value of pursuing the same phenomenon through a number of societies which belong to the same genre such as are found in the interlacustrine region.

Southern Busoga followed the same pattern of development as Buganda. This is notwithstanding the fact that up to the time of colonial intervention Busoga was still ruled by kinglets who, although had by and large taken control of the land, had not yet completely eliminated competition over distribution of land from heads of lineages. But the principle of chiefly estates or administrative domains had been firmly established along the same lines as Buganda. In contrast to Buganda and Busoga (south), which were hundred per cent agricultural, in the other interlacustrine kingdoms pastoralism was the dominant mode of production. To complicate matters further, from the point of view of land tenure, most of this was not only nomadic but was combined with agriculture practised by the majority of the population, the so-called Bairu. In Bunyoro and Toro, although there is frequent reference in the literature to estates given to chiefs or district governors by the king, there is no evidence that the *Omukama* (King) had "eaten up" the whole country as in Buganda. On the contrary, there are indications that the principle of usufruct rights under lineage supervision survived outside official estates.

Even within such administrative domains, it is apparent that the object of control was not land but rather people and cattle. The role of cattle, as a prestige good, is obvious. But cattle had to be tended and protected from raids. The patron-client relationship met this requirement. Those who sought cattle to improve their social and economic standing attached themselves as suppliants to wealthy cattle-owners or chiefs. It should be noted here that all big cattle-owners, whether chiefs or not, enjoyed great social prestige and were identified as *Bahuma* - a special "aristocratic stratum". In the previous chapter we dismissed the idea that they were a caste. An aristocracy they might have been.

Unlike land in Buganda, cattle in Bunyoro and elsewhere in the interlacustrine remained a heritable family asset. Secondly, they were liable to unlimited accumulation by well-placed individuals. The chiefs, like the *Omukama*, collected dues and tribute from their tenants. Beattie reports that:

> One of the first things a chief does on appointment is to acquire a tenanted estate ... in some populated area not already claimed by somebody else[3].

Apart from dues and tribute, the chiefs in Bunyoro and Toro extracted succession, marriage, burial and grazing fees. These were not limited only to perishable goods as in Buganda. They included the prized item, cattle. In addition to this, Beattie maintains that in Bunyoro chiefship

> Was not just a formal administrative office rather, it was a private and personal (though conditional) possession, which like any other private property was thought of as hereditable[4].

Beattie believes that a very large part of populated Bunyoro had been taken up by these *de facto* private estates, even though the *Omukama* reserved the right to confirm or refuse succession to official estates. What emerges, therefore, from this account is a property-owning class in Bunyoro which was capable of reproducing itself - something which could not be said of Buganda. The question now is whether or not this class constituted a landed aristocracy.

Beattie has described this as a "feudal" aristocracy. Short of extreme formalism, it cannot be denied that much land in Bunyoro was held in feud on a more or less permanent basis. It is also clear that chiefs and other

---

3   Beattie, 1961, p. 39.
4   Op. cit., p. 36.

Bahuma patrons received services and economic value from their clients. But they did this more as loyal suppliants than serfs. As in Buganda, there was no bondage. The clients did not see themselves as a labouring class beholden to particular proprietors but rather as loyal followers or clients who rendered public or private services to the chief or patron, without losing their autonomy as producers. Once again, Beattie refers to this class as "peasants" *Bairu* in exactly the same way they were referred to as *bakopi* in Buganda. But neither had independent tenure or use rights, unlike those producers who remained within the lineage system. It would appear then that while property-relations in Bunyoro were symptomatic of a feudal system, production relations did not tally with this. What are these tenant cultivators to be called? Furthermore, does the division between agriculture and pastoralism, both of which were associated with distinct classes in Bunyoro, amount to a juxtaposition of two modes of production or interchangeable modes of existence? Suffice it to say for the time being, it transpires that, despite the differences in the superstructure in favour of Buganda, processes of class-formation were far more advanced in Bunyoro than in Buganda.

Even at the level of productive forces it seems that Bunyoro-Kitara had a head-start on Buganda. It would be remembered that it was there that the first iron-smelting in the interlacustrine region occurred. The production of iron-ore and agricultural implements such as hoes and knives of varying sizes was an important step, not to say anything about the forging of iron weapons which must have helped Bunyoro build her vast empire. Secondly, the discovery of salt centres in Bunyoro led to a flourishing trade over a fairly large area. The development of early markets, supplied with domestically produced goods, was unusual in the region. Buganda at its zenith only managed to add barkcloth to the list. Both in Bunyoro and in Buganda specialist producers were subject to control by the king and his chiefs and were generally accorded a low status. While there is no evidence that in Bunyoro, as in Buganda, the producers suffered onerous exactions, it is evident that there was more intensive exploitation of internal labour in Bunyoro than in Buganda. But, as in Buganda, the main objective was to provide utilities for the chiefs and the Bahuma in general, unless cattle are seen as a form of investment in a semi-pastoral economy. Indeed, the question of whether cattle in these circumstances represent capital or something else will best be illuminated by an analysis of the predominantly pastoral economies of the south-western kingdoms of Ankore, Rwanda and Burundi.

In Ankore, Rwanda and Burundi there was a sharper division between pastoralists and agriculturalists than, say, in Bunyoro, Buhaya, Buzinza and Buha. This was accounted for by a conscious attempt on the part of the dominant pastoralists to limit access among agriculturalists only to unproductive cattle. This was reinforced by an ideology which drew invidious distinctions between what was supposed to be separate ethnic groups, the Bahima and the Bairu. This was given substance by a semi-endogamous system. The Bairu men were not allowed to cohabit with Bahima women, whereas Bahima lords (including kings) often kept Bairu concubines. Willy-nilly, this gave rise to a situation wherein the status of some Bairu got improved through their mothers and fuller participation in pastoralism became possible. However, what is germane to our discussion is the fact that two modes of existence prevailed concurrently, irrespective of who participated in them. Secondly, there is no doubt that one mode was subordinate to the other and that the people who were responsible for it were accorded an inferior status, "Bairu", that is to say, non-pastoralists. This became an obstensible ground for excluding them from political power, at least, in Ankore and Rwanda. However, this should not be confused with ethnic categories or separate modes of production, as Bonte did in his basically Althusserian study, "Marxist Theory and Anthropological Analysis"[5].

We have already rejected the theory of Bairu versus Bahima as ideological i.e. it is more of a justification than an explanation. In our view, the real explanation resides in production and property relations. Nevertheless, this is not as self-evident as a number of Marxists are inclined to think. First, on the question of property rights: in all three kingdoms land, the most basic resource, does not seem to have been an issue. Neither the Bairu nor their overlords, the Bahima/Batutsi, strived to stake a personal and permanent claim on land. The emphasis on both sides was on usufruct rights. Even the *Omugabe* or *Omwami* who both treated the whole kingdom as their foot-stool had no greater claim on land as a resource than they did on cattle which belonged to individual families. In an interesting text on Rwanda Maquet otherwise an ardent believer in feudalism in Rwanda, observes that:

> On each pasture, cultivated plot or forest area, the king had a right very similar to the *dominion eminens* of Roman law, the kind of public ownership that a state has over the land within the borders[6].

This is to say that the king had over land a right potentially superior to that of anyone else. But Maquet concludes significantly enough that:

---

5   Bonte, P., *Marxist Theory and Anthropological Analysis* in Kahn and Llobera, 1981.
6   Maquet, J., *The Premise of Inequality in Rwanda*, London, 1961, p. 90.

In fact, the king very rarely insisted on this use of his rights and then only when he wanted to punish somebody who was guilty of disobedience or of some other crime[7].

Likewise, a global right over all cattle in Rwanda was the privilege of the king which he used, as Maquet reports, "against important chiefs who might indulge in intrigues against him". Therefore, the idea that the *Omugabe* or *Omwami* "owned" all the land and cattle in his kingdom should be treated as an expression of suzerainty over the territory and its people. This is in sharp contrast to what we saw in Buganda and Bunyoro, where there was substantive royal control over land as well as property in land in the case of Bunyoro.

However, the BanyAnkore and Watutsi kings, like the Baganda and Banyoro kings, handed out fiefdoms to their territorial chiefs and political favourites. Like the king, the incumbents were entitled to tribute from their subjects in the form of cattle products and sometimes cattle from the Bahima pastoralists and beer and other agricultural products from the Bairu or Bahutu. In addition, they were entitled to a share of the dues collected by land or cattle chiefs from within their domains. As in Bunyoro, political offices were in theory appointive but in practice could be handed down with the consent of the sovereign. Unlike in Bunyoro, this had no implications of ownership of land on the part of the incumbent. The general rule was usufruct rights for purposes of cultivation which were vested in family heads. In northern Rwanda the land was thought of as belonging to patrilineages, despite the suzerainty of the *Omwami*. Therefore, we are left with a situation where ownership was limited only to cattle. Even this right was compromised by well-established usufructuary rights, which is a fairly common practice among pastoralists in Africa. As far as one can see, these rights fall within the sphere of production relations. First of all, let it be noted that, while the Bahima and Batutsi by virtue of being identified with the rulers enjoyed social prestige, this did not necessarily imply different labour processes in agriculture and in pastoralism. In agriculture the Bairu and Bahutu, relied on their own labour for cultivation, but shared the produce with their pastoral overlords in the form of tribute and dues. Nonetheless, they maintained their autonomy as producers under the usufruct system. The same is true of the ordinary Bahima/Batutsi pastoralists. They had free access to pastures to graze their own herds, as long as they paid allegiance to the king and the territorial chief in whose domain they resided. Payment

7   Ibid.

of dues and tribute signified allegiance to the chief. Among the herdsmen and the cultivators there was voluntary exchange of pastoral and agricultural products. This could legitimately be referred to as a symbiotic relationship, since it did not involve any exploitation or compulsion. However, the same is not true of the relationship between the rulers and the producers. The king and his staff extracted economic value from the producers in the form of tribute and dues. In the case of the pastoralists these consisted of cattle and fresh milk. The cultivators delivered normally fixed proportions of their produce. Over and above this, the Bairu and the Bahutu were liable to labour dues which, as in Buganda and Bunyoro, were limited to public works such as building roads, building or mending chiefs' enclosures and carrying supplies during expeditions. In contradistinction, the Bahima and the Batutsi commoners were liable only to military services, something which was consistent with their general social prestige and the habitual cattle raids among pastoralists.

Apart from the king and his chiefs, there was a non-producing class in Ankore, Rwanda and Burundi. This compromised of wealthy cattle owners, who depended on the services of those who were in need of cattle or protection. The latter were largely drawn from among the cultivators, though not exclusively. We are here referring to the well-known patron-client relationship which got highly elaborated in the pastoral kingdoms in question and which had started in Bunyoro outside the official bureaucracy. This is a relationship of great inequality which at the same time gives rise to usufruct rights in cattle. This is highlighted by the dramatic expression used by the would-be-clients in Rwanda: "Give me milk; make me rich; be my father" *urampe amata, urankize, urambere umubyeyi*. If agreeable, the patron bestowed upon his client a few beasts over whose milk and male progeny he had full rights. The female offspring remained the property of the patron, which was a sure way of preventing any accumulation on the part of the client. In addition, the patron was expected to offer political protection, a helping hand to his client in times of hardship or in ritual ceremonies such as weddings and funerals; in cases of crime, blood feud or any other predicament. Finally, depending on the relationship, the patron was supposed to take interest in the general well-being of his client and family even after the client's death, should there be no family members to look after them. This was a paternalistic relationship which acted as a substitute for the usual kinship relations. It muffled class contradictions and played an important role in the ideological reproduction of political power.

It also constituted direct exploitation of the labour power of the client, but once again not as intensely as could be expected. Apart from minding the patron's herds two or three days a week or working in the fields for an equivalent number of days to produce agricultural goods for the use of the patron, clients spent a greater part of their time doing menial jobs for the patron such as accompanying him when he goes on a journey or to the king's or chief's court, keeping his residence and enclosures in good repair or simply holding the beer-calabash while his lordship imbibed. As can be seen, the fiscal policy of the pastoral kingdoms was aimed mainly at providing perishable consumer goods and personal services for royalty, the bureaucracy and a small *pastoral* aristocracy. It is a serious mistake to talk of a Bahima or Batutsi aristocracy, for the majority of the Bahima or Batutsi were not lords who owned large herds of cattle. Instead, the majority of them managed their own modest herds of cattle for their own benefit. It is true that by virtue of their social prestige they were exempted from certain labour-dues, but for the greater part they had nothing to do with the court. Some continued with their nomadic lives across the border in search of new pastures.

Although writers such as Lemarchand believe that the clients in Rwanda and Burundi (and by extension Ankore) contracted patronage because they had no alternative, there are no compelling grounds for accepting this suggestion. In so far as there was no seizure of the land by Omugabe or Omwami in Ankore and Rwanda/Burundi unlike in Buganda, and in so far as there was no property in land in these kingdoms, the direct producers, the cultivators and the herdsmen, had not been expropriated. But in so far as the king had suzerainty over the whole territory and his governors over given domains, the producers were liable to political control not so much as labouring tenants but rather as subjects. In conformity with the latter, they were obliged to pay tax, tribute and labour-dues. Beyond this, they were not obligated to anybody. Then why patronage? Our hunch is that patronage was a personal arrangement which reflected lack of political representation among the subordinate classes or of a desire for prestige goods (i.e. cattle) rather than an outright economic necessity. There is no evidence that the clients in Ankore, Rwanda and Burundi received from their patrons more value than they gave. In Buganda the advantage was that clients gained access to land which otherwise was out of their reach.

Once again, it does not seem that in the kingdoms under consideration there was feud in cattle either. Governors or chiefs received no cattle by virtue of their appointment to high office. Instead, they gave cattle to the king as tribute, which would imply that they were in turn the king's clients. Therefore, the idea of a "feudal aristocracy" in these kingdoms must be rejected in favour of a more appropriate concept. Those who owned large herds of cattle, who enjoyed prestige and power, and commanded the services and the loyalty of others could be accurately referred to as a *pastoral aristocracy.* This is even more so when we recall that in the pastoral kingdoms accumulation of cattle was not a result of sustained exploitation of labour. It was a natural process which gave a political advantage to a few individuals. Technology remained rudimentary and the technical conditions for social reproduction were indistinguishable from those found in tribal societies. No markets existed and utility value predominated. However, the rest of the pastoralists as much as the cultivators constituted a class of producers who were dominated by a pastoral aristocracy. As a corollary to this, it is arguable that agriculture and pastoralism not only complemented each other but were integrated into a single mode of production for the sake of meeting the needs of this pastoral aristocracy. If the Bahima and Batutsi were exempted from certain chores for ideological reasons, the more numerous cultivators became serviceable in both agriculture and in animal husbandry. The ultimate logic of this is revealed by the historical experience of Buhaya, Buzinza and Buha where pastoralism and agriculture got combined in the same hands.

In Buzinza and Buha, where some of the Batutsi nomadic pastoralists migrated from Rwanda and Burundi, there is no evidence of a pastoral aristocracy. Instead, there are signs that a mixed economy developed, involving Batutsi/Bahuma as well as Bairu. It was, as we argued in the last chapter, a tribal economy in which the lineage principle was dominant. Individual producers gained access to land and cattle through their minimal lineages. However, as is true of tribal organization, a certain hierarchy existed among the various clans and lineages and within them. At the top there were the ruling Bahinda clans. The commoner Bahinda, Batutsi and mixed or eminent Bairu clans enjoyed less prestige than the former but more than the rest of the population which consisted mainly of Bairu clans. As far as access to land was concerned, these status differences seem to have been immaterial. Chiefs had only dominion over territory and were entitled to the usual gifts which cannot, properly-speaking, be referred to as tribute. Any contrary claim would be unwarranted, as the chief did not stand in a relation of a patron or lord to the ordinary citizens. He was merely first among equals and under the redistributory tribal system, he was expected to give as much as he received. Failure to do so could cost him his chieftainship, as he would lose support to one of his lineage rivals.

In contrast, in Buhaya kinglets laid claim to most of the land and reserved the right to give out estates as fiefs *nyarubanja* to their appointed chiefs as well as to royal princes who were deliberately kept out of power. All the peasants and herders who were settled on these estates became tenants of the fief-holders and owed them tribute and labour-dues. Nonetheless, as elsewhere in the interlacustrine region, they were not bonded. In Buhaya, as in Bunyoro and unlike in Buganda, greater personal than public services were expected of tenants. Furthermore, although in theory official estates were not heritable, in practice they often got inherited with the approval of the king *Omukama*. In fact, the king had the right to create hereditable estates (an act known as *kwehonga*). The exactions on the tenants might not have been onerous, but it is apparent that private appropriation of land and economic value from the direct producers had become a fact of life. However, like in all the other kingdoms (except Buganda), the system had not yet become exclusive. Within it there remained some land under the effective control of lineage heads, who apportioned it according to customary usufruct rights. This not to the contrary, it can be concluded that at the level of property relations there was semblance of feudalism in Buhaya, as in Bunyoro. There was a growing *landed aristocracy*. But production-relations, as elsewhere in the interlacustrine, were still dominated by patron-client relations whose connotations were more political than economic. Perhaps, a distinction ought to be made in such instances between exploitation of subjects and exploitation of labour. These might signify different modes of production, and different kinds of value. In this regard the term, "economic surplus" is not only useless but is also a misconception since we cannot tell what is surplus and what is not.

PHYSICAL PRODUCTION AND ORGANIZATION OF LABOUR

People enter into production relations and appropriate nature with the purpose of producing specific goods. While the choice of goods is peculiar to each society, the range of possibilities is influenced by ecological conditions, at least in natural economies. Details of what Africans produced for themselves are generally unknown to or taken for granted by most social scientists, with the exception of geographers, agriculturalists and economists. In the case of the latter two oftentimes though known, traditional crops tended to be ignored in favour of those crops which had commercial value. Yet, with the recent crises in African agriculture, researchers as well as policy-makers are beginning to ask themselves questions about what went wrong. Humanistic social sciences such as history and anthropology which should provide the necessary background are particularly weak in this area. The main reason is that, conventionally, this is treated as a technical field. Yet, the division of knowledge into air-tight compartments is becoming something of the past, especially in underdeveloped countries where agrarian questions are overriding. Concrete as our analysis of production relations has been, it did not amount to a sustained discussion of what the people of the interlacustrine region actually produced.

The interlacustrine region falls into two main ecological zones: rain-forest zone on the lake shores where elephant grass and plantains flourish; and the savannah or short grass zone suitable for cattle raising and grain cultivation. The weather is equitable. Two rainy seasons - one long and one short - alternate with two dry seasons of equivalent lengths. This makes it possible for two crops to be grown each year. Within the rain-forest zone plantains *Musa sapientum* are universally the staple crop. Banana, as a permanent crop, allowed for settled agriculture in the region from the earliest times. It also meant relatively easy work for the producers, as plantains have heavy yields (4-6 tons per acre/year) and can keep producing for up to thirty years. Secondly, their own discarded leaves act as mulch and compost. No seeds are needed, as reproduction is by vegetative propagation. Banana groves average about 3 acres and it is believed that one woman was sufficient to maintain one grove. With a few exceptions, banana cultivation was the responsibility of women. In the short grass zone small millet *Eleusine coracana* was the staple crop. In contrast to the banana, it had much lighter yields (900-1800 lbs of grain per acre per year). It required more extensive cultivation (5-8 acres). It was difficult to store and liable to attack by weevils *Cosmopolites sordidus*. It is obvious that millet required a great deal of labour and was destined to be displaced by grain-crops which promised heavier yields for the same amount of work, for example, maize. Of course, this was at the risk of leaching the light tropical soils, as we know now. It seems that, although both men and women participated in grain cultivation, the greater burden fell on women. As has been shown, in the interlacustrine region men were often required to serve their patrons, to herd cattle and to join military expeditions. It might have been precisely this division of labour which led to the separation between cash and subsistence crops during the colonial era. Men were required to serve their new masters in the modern sector, while relegating women, the undisputed food producers, to the background - a factor which had serious implications for the future.

A variety of supplementary crops were grown in the region. Among these, cassava *Manihot utilissima* ranked highest with yields of 3-6 tons per acre per year and highly adaptable to different climatic conditions. Sweet potatoes, although not as adaptable, were an important addition yielding 2-6 tons per acre per year. Ground nuts *Arachis hypogea* were common and did well in the lighter tropical soils (yields, 600-800 lbs per acre per year). Grown in relatively small quantities were crops such as simsim, beans, peas, chilles, pumpkins, gourds, okra, onions and even ginger. Most of these crops did very well in the region, especially in the wetter zone around the lakes. The point of enumerating them is to show that the idea of mono-culturalism is alien to African cultivators. The second intention is to demonstrate that the frequent charge by the colonial authorities and their successors that African peasants are conservative are, historically, unjustified. In pre-colonial times the interlacustrians adopted a number of crops from outside. These include the famous plantain, sweet potatoes *Ipomea batatas*, peas *Pisum sativum*, beans *Phaseolus* and maize *Zea mays*, which reached Uganda in the 1860s[8].

As can be seen, agriculture was less secure in the short grass zone. In contrast, cattle did best there. Therefore, pastoralism should be regarded, not as in competition with agriculture but as complementary to it. If the introduction of cattle in these areas was accidental, then their adoption was not, one would surmise. Under these conditions cattle must have offered another opportunity for diversification of production. In other words, they became a prestige good only by association. In central and southern Africa where other Bantu-speakers settled and where comparable ecological conditions obtained, a mixture of pastoralism and arable agriculture became the general rule. Moreover, unlike in the pastoral kingdoms of the interlacustrine region, the two were combined in the hands of the same producers. Thus, ownership of cattle, except in large numbers, was not a mark of distinction as was the case among the Bahuma, Bahima or Batutsi. However, it is important to note that among all these people the economic value of cattle was not in their meat but mainly in their dairy products and in the social reproduction of lineage groups. Cattle were given in exchange for women in societies in which clan exogamy was the norm. Otherwise, animal husbandry remained traditional. The famed long-horned *nganda* cattle of the interlacustrine region have very little body flesh and their milk yields hardly exceeded a maximum of 1.5 litters per cow per day. Numbers compensated for quality, something which could not be maintained indefinitely, given increasing demographic pressure on the land. In agriculture the situation was not any better. The technological level was very low, the hoe and the adze being the main tools for production. while in the plantain zone alluvial soils of up to fourteen feet deep made shifting cultivation unnecessary, whatever intensive cultivation that might have occurred did not represent intensification of technological factors. In the less fertile short grass zone extensive and shifting cultivation were the

---

8   See Konczacki, Z.A. & J.M. (eds), *An Economic History of Black Africa*, London, 1977; pp. 41-51.

standard practice and the same technology was used. In other words, it was possible to increase or maintain the volume of production, without increasing labour productivity. To a very large extent the producers depended on nature's bounty: in one case it was soil fertility and in the other it was the general abundance of land. Hardly any rotational farming had been introduced, the plough which had come as far south as Ethiopia and the Sudan had not been adopted and, despite the existence of large numbers of oxen, no animal traction was practised. Likewise, despite the fact that cotton *Gossypium* grew wild in many parts of the region, no spinning and weaving had been reported, except for simple girdles for women. Hides and barkcloth were used for clothing. It is as if the Africans in the region had played into the hands of their worst detractors, and yet not.

The state of the arts in a society is a reflection of its level of social development. Whatever our predispositions, in this day and age it would be errant nonsense to suppose that the peoples of the interlacustrine failed to adopt what had become common knowledge elsewhere out of ignorance or stupidity. Indeed, explorers' and colonial reports are full of praises for such peoples as the Baganda and Batutsi for their intelligence and political astuteness. It is as if the founders of the interlacustrine kingdoms had been put on pedestal so as to be condemned, the more the crueller. Subjective reactions aside, it may be pointed out that, in contrast to the plough and the wheel, the adoption of certain crops from Asia, from the New World and Europe was as fast as could be expected so was it with cattle. All these must have coincided with perceived needs. Technologies remained within the confines of these needs, despite the advent of the iron age in Bunyoro and later in Buganda. Craftsmen limited themselves to the production of hoes, spears, knives, adzes, leather-tanning, barkcloth and canoes in Buganda. Kings' palaces, though elaborate and filled with aristocratic airs, consisted of primitive structures made of wattle and daub crowned with thatched roofs - all too basic to lay foundations for advanced civilization.

This is to be expected. The interlacustrine kingdoms were young societies which, nevertheless had developed fairly rapidly within their context. This is particularly true of Buganda. But even in her case when the roll is called, she would have very little to show, apart from her bureaucracy and military organization. For those monarchs who survived on milk and butter like *Omugabe* of Ankore and the *Omwami* of Rwanda or Burundi the scores are even lower. But the point to grasp is that, as long as their needs were met, they had no reason to struggle. The land was plentiful, the herds numerous and supplies from agriculture ample. Under these conditions even the need to intensify the exploitation of labour did not exist. Before they could have thought of introducing the plough so as to increase production, the rulers of the interlacustrine kingdoms might have thought of first converting their tribute-paying subjects into servile labour or serfs. Instead, they raided their neighbour for extra value, as we are told by Marxists historians such as Coquery-Vidrovitch and liberal historians such as Wrigley who described Buganda as "an economy of predation rather than production". The overall political situation and the objective material conditions in the region would suggest otherwise. Buganda or any of the other kingdoms could not have been raiding its neighbour in search of extra value any more than did the pastoralists when they raided one another. In so far as all the interlacustrine kingdoms were at this stage committed to utility value, there is nothing they could have hoped to get from their neighbour which they did not already have or could not have obtained internally. Women and male captives, who seem to have been the main asset, were turned into concubines and domestic slaves who were quickly assimilated into the local population. The rest were perishable goods which added nothing significant to the domestic supply. Therefore, our conclusion is that these raids were carried out mainly to expand territory or political hegemony over weaker kingdoms. Once the latter had been achieved there were no more raids, but tribute which in principle was no different from that which was collected from local subordinate chiefs and clients. In other words, accumulation and conversion was still the problem of these societies. This was most acute in the pastoral kingdoms which simply collapsed under the impact of capitalism and whose erstwhile aristocracies were swept aside as symbols of darkness. Witness the dramatic changes in the late 1950s and in the 1960s in Rwanda, Burundi and Ankore.

The development of markets is thought by many to facilitate the processes of accumulation and conversion of values. This is true but not inevitable. It appears that the purpose of production is the determining factor. If the primary purpose is to maximize utility value, there might be no development beyond a certain level of accumulation. Perhaps, it is for this reason that long-distance trade has been seen by economic historians and Marxists as the key to the problem. Apart from a number of historical analogies, for example, Europe and the East, even this does not seem to be inevitable as is evinced by the history of the interlacustrine kingdoms. Most of them had no markets but simple barter. However, as had been mentioned, Bunyoro had developed early markets, trading in salt, simple iron tools and tanned leather. By the late 18th century Buganda and Busoga had followed suit, as is reported by Kiwanuka:

> The people of Kyagwe used to trade with islanders of Buvuma, Bugaya, Lwaaje and Koome in goats, fish, sheep, barkcloth, dried foods and even cattle. Their markets, which extended from Bukunja to Bulongoganyi,

were famous and used to attract large concourses of people. The Basoga traded with the Samia in the East, the Bagisu in the north, the Banyara and Buruli in the north-west and of course with the people of Eastern Kyagwe[9].

The temptation to make whatever was happening at this point in time sound big has to be resisted. Buganda, despite its political and military vigour, had in fact not advanced much in its development of productive forces. Nor did it show a level of accumulation which held good prospects for such a breakthrough.? In this respect, it was as backwards as any of the interlacustrine kingdoms. It might be that Johnston's imperialist outburst at the turn of this century that "Baganda chiefs were only 10 years and two pieces of barkcloth ahead of the Wakavirondo" was not unfounded. It must be conceded that the existence of short-distance markets in the few interlacustrine kingdoms led neither to significant levels of accumulation nor to intensification of productive forces. Utility value continued to govern all production.

They only question that remains now is whether or not long-distance trade played its classical role in the interlacustrine region. Although long-distance trade did not start in earnest in the interlacustrine region until the middle of the 19th century, there is evidence that by the end of the 18th century some exotic goods had reached the region by way of Karagwe. According to Thomas and Scott, these included cups and plates, dark blue cotton cloth, copper wire and cowrie shells. Trade remained sporadic until 1840 when the Sultan of Oman, Seyyied Said, moved his capital to Zanzibar in agreement with the British. Thereafter, caravans journeyed more regularly from Zanzibar to Moshi and Arusha, and then across to Tabora and Ujiji and thence north to the interlacustrine kingdoms. Buzinza benefited from the trade mainly because it was on the direct route to the north. But the two kingdoms which were competing for the control of long-distance trade, as would be expected, were Buganda and Bungoro. However, what is of particular interest to us is the nature of the merchandise itself. It turns out that all that came from Zanzibar was firearms, cotton and a variety of trinkets. In exchange the Arab traders bought ivory and slaves from the Africans. For strategic reasons the king of Buganda found it necessary to control all trade. Kiwanuka boasts that:

---

9   Kiwanuka, op. cit., p. 151.

By the third of the 19th century, the Baganda were equipping their own caravans for long-distance trade to the east coast. The main commodity was ivory and some slaves[10].

Furthermore, he believes that

The securing of the south-west trade route through Buddu to Kiziba, which indirectly linked Buganda with the east, was a development of momentous results[11].

What results, it may be asked. Both ivory and slaves were wasting resources and, above all, were no measure of the productive capacity of Buganda. Neither were the guns, cloth and trinkets bought through the sale of these commodities a great technological investment. The Banyoro kings did not fare any better. Having created a similar trade monopoly in guns and ivory, they showed no investment in technology or production. Even the guns ended up being used for civil wars or fatricidal fights for the benefit of British imperialism towards the end of the 19th century. Hence, Thomas and Scott, with typical cynicism, remark that during this period

Trade, in fact, was still a not unromantic trafficking in ivory and gew-gaws, to which slaves, gunpowder, and rifles occasionally contributed an illicit fermentative element[12].

The verdict is clear. Like short-distance trade, long-distance trade led neither to capital accumulation nor to technological investment or increased production relying on existing technologies. Instead, it led to some drainage of existing manpower, which could have been used otherwise. Putting aside the whys and wherefores, what is to be borne in mind for the time being is that even so there was hardly any dislocation from the point of view of maintaining utility value. This has profound theoretical implications, as will be shown in the next chapter.

Suffice it to say, British imperialism reacted to the situation by devising methods to stimulate trade. One of these was an announcement by the British Acting Commissioner in Uganda in the Zanzibar Gazette of 4th October 1989 that:

---

10   Kiwanuka, op. cit., p. 151.
11   Ibid.
12   Thomas and Scott, *Uganda*, London, 1935, p. 343.

English cloth (similar to Amerikani ...), cheap looking-glasses, gaudy waistcoats, pocket knives, scissors, enamelled iron-ware, cheap clocks and watches, beads, brass wire, coloured blankets, cheap jewellery, tarbooshes and Arab coats would find a ready market in the Uganda protectorate[13].

In other words, the interlacustrine societies were being turned into markets for British manufactures before they had discovered their own capacity to produce goods for exchange. It was freely acknowledged by British spokesmen such as Lord Lugard that the scramble for Africa by the nations of Europe was due to growing commercial rivalry, which brought home to the civilized nations the vital necessity of securing the only remaining fields for industrial enterprise and expansion. He actually warned that:

It is well, then, to realize that it is for our advantage ... that we have undertaken responsibilities in East Africa. It is in order to foster growth of trade of this country, and to find an outlet for our manufactures and our surplus energy (surplus population) ...[14].

The interlacustrine kingdoms were hardly prepared for such an onslaught. Militarily and politically, their leaders resisted colonial penetration as much as they could. But political fragmentation of the regional social formation made it easy for the British to take it piecemeal. Consequently, some capitulated and turned against their neighbour, for example, when Buganda joined British forces against Kabarega, the king of Bunyoro, who fought to the bitter end. Thereafter, it was a matter of months before the British (and the Belgian in the south-west) took over the economies in the region and incorporated them into the capitalist system. This was done by introducing cash crops more or less on mandatory terms at the beginning of this century. Cotton (*Gossypium hirsutum* from America) and coffee *(robusta* and *arabica*, depending on the altitude).

This meant a definite substitution of exchange value for the original utility value which characterized the economies of the region. Because of the emphasis on cash-crops, the agriculturalists managed to adapt. For the pastoralists, it meant complete abandonment not only of their means of livelihood but also of their way of life, something they resisted strenuously

---

13   Thomas and Scott, op. cit., p. 343.
14   Lugard, F.D., *The Rise of Our East African Empire*, London, 1893, p. 391). As quoted in Karugire, op. cit., p. 53.

but to no avail. Their supremacy in all the kingdoms was shattered remorselessly. With the jettisoning of utility value, subsistence production also suffered neglect. One cannot help but see a parallel here between pastoralism and subsistence agriculture. It would seem that under pastoralism cattle are as much of an instrument of production as land is under the usufruct system. Therefore, both pastoralists and subsistence cultivators suffered under capitalism because of the inability or unwillingness to convert their instruments of production into capital which, if lucky, could have brought them added value but which most probably would have escaped them, given their economic uncompetitiveness.

Therefore, there is a logic behind the conservatism of this class of producers. It is precisely that logic which capitalism, according to classical theory whether Marxist or non-Marxist, is meant to destroy. This harks back to Samir Amin's thesis that capitalism is a necessary stage because it is the only way in which productive forces could be developed further in economies in which utility value predominates. The Chinese socialist experience, which Samir Amin cherishes, would cast doubt on this theoretical supposition. Secondly, on ideological grounds he would be hard put to justify the rape of the peasantry by capital, especially in the Third World. The fundamental question though is whether the requisite technological conditions for development are inextricably bound with particular modes of production or historical stages. Under capitalism this has been the case. But is it inevitable? The relationship between economics, politics and ideology deserves our closest attention, especially in societies in transition. The history of the interlacustrine kingdoms shows a certain latitude in the way these things fit together and also shows that modes of production do not have to be complete to exist. Or are we destined for a proliferation of modes of production? These are some of the questions we hope to answer in the next chapter.

THE "TRIBUTARY" MODE IN THE INTERLACUSTRINE: REFLEC-TIONS ON AN HYPOTHESIS

It seems indisputable that the foundations of every society are economic. In order to survive people have to provide for themselves goods and services. Whether this is in the final analysis determinant of all social existence is an issue on which liberals and Marxists are irreconcilably opposed. But it would appear that the reasons for such a polarization are more ideological than scientific. Bourgeois economists have over a period of two hundred years treated economic growth as an unexceptionable index of social development. If this were not the case, the idea of positive economics and classification of societies according to the size of their GNP or income *per caput* would not have been the sticking points in modern development theory. In reality bourgeois economists no less than Marxists put a primacy on the economic factor. The difference, however, is in the way in which that is conceptualized. Bourgeois theorists make it appear that economic self-interest or avarice is the driving force behind development, whereas Marxists attribute development to impersonal material forces. The latter view makes it possible to decode social systems and to classify them according to some abstract principles such as "mode of production". Like the natural theology of the bourgeois economists, concepts such as "mode of production" have universalistic pretensions. In recent years these pretensions have been subjected to severe tests by confronting them with the historical reality of regions outside Europe.

In Africa the initial tendency had been to search for an African mode of production[1]. This was particularly aimed at forestalling an earlier attempt by Marxist historians such as Suret-Canale[2] to extend the so-called Asiatic mode of production to Africa. Those concerned had become vaguely aware

1   Coquery-Vidrovitch, C., *Research on an African Mode of Production* in Seddon (ed.), 1978 (first published in French in 1969).
2   Suret-Canale, J., *Les Sociétiés Traditionelles en Afrique Tropicale et le Concept de Mode de Production Asiatique*, 1964.

of the peculiarities of African social formations. Meillassoux was the first one to carry out concrete studies on the problem and to introduce new notions such as "self-sustaining agricultural societies" and the "lineage mode of production"[3]. In subsequent debates and research his ideas proved to be seminal, as will be shown later. Nonetheless, the debate remained inconclusive until Samir Amin's vigorous intervention in the early seventies. He rejected outrightly the idea of extending either the "Asiatic mode of production" or "feudalism" to Africa. He maintained that the former was a product of Eurocentrism and had neither historical nor scientific validity. Likewise, he argued that feudalism, far from being universal, was peculiar to Europe. At best, it was an incomplete stage of a more general mode of production, namely, *the tributary mode of production*, by which he sought to replace both feudalism and the Asiatic mode of production. These ideas found full expression in his book, *Class and Nation, Historically and in the Current Crisis*[4]. It will be more than interesting to check them against the interlacustrine social formations, to some of which Amin himself has made constant reference (e.g. Buganda and Rwanda).

Before we embark on this it might be opportune to register here that, whereas at an earlier stage the anthropologists who worked in the region had taken for granted the existence of "feudalism" among the interlacustrines, by the beginning of the sixties some of them had, like Amin, become sceptical. This turned on three major points of comparison, viz., dependent land tenure between vassal and lord, territorial autonomy of feudal lords within the state, and the organization of agricultural production. On all three counts the interlacustrine social formations were markedly different from European feudal societies. In feudal Europe, the relationship of men to land was one of the main determinants of political and social status. The feudal lord's possession and disposition of property rights gave a permanence to the relationship between him and his vassals or serfs. In the interlacustrine kingdoms this was not the case, even in Bunyoro and Buhaya where the nearest thing to fiefdoms existed. The tenants were not bonded and in principle office estates were not heritable. This would suggest absence of property-relations in land. Secondly, the dispersal of political authority through autonomous landlords which was characteristic of feudal Europe did not exist in the interlacustrine kingdoms. The opposite was the case.

---

3   Meillassoux, C., *La Phenomene Economique dans le Sociétés Traditionalles d'Autosubsistence*, 1960; *Anthropologie Economique des Gouro de Cote d'Ivoire*, The Hague, 1964; and *From Reproduction to Production*, Economy and Society, 1972.

4   Amin Samir, *Classs and Nation Historically and in the Current Crisis*, N.Y., 1980.

Thirdly, whereas in feudal Europe the seigniorial mode of estate management was an important source of private wealth, in the interlacustrine kingdoms the idea of a lord's demesne cultivated by the corvee labour of bonded tenants did not exist. Instead, office estate-holders relied on the labour of their wives and domestic slaves for subsistence production. It was in view of these and other differences that Goody, writing ten years later, was prompted to state that:

> There seems even less to be gained from adopting the view which sees African societies as feudalities on the basis of wider political or economic criteria. Firstly, there is the ever-present ambiguity of the term itself; and then again the primary referent is to a particular period in European history, and an author employing an analytic tool of this kind tends to focus the whole analysis around the Western situation. The difficulties are nowhere clearer than in the writings of those who see the development of human society in terms of the stages so widely used in the latter half of the nineteenth century[5].

Goody was not alone or even the first one to express such misgivings. In the final chapter of the *East African Chiefs*, E.M. Chilver, a specialist on medieval history, had observed that:

> Historians, in their capacity as biographers of institutions, are disinclined to use terminologies derived from one culture and period to describe institutions in others. As I hope I have shown, analogies often do as much violence to the example as to the parallel. 'Feudalism', half a millenium of it, has to be caricatured to be contrasted with other ways of ordering political relations. Interlacustrine Bantu institutions must be deprived of their personality if they are to be presented divorced from the sentiments which surround them. But perhaps the analogies and contrasts will have served some purpose if it can be established that the interlacustrine kingdoms and the states of feudal Europe *differ markedly from one another in political structure and that estates granted to office-holders to maintain or reward them are not fiefs, but office lands* - emphasis added[6].

If there was the danger of throwing out the baby with the bath-water, Goody warned that:

---

5   Goody, J., *Technology, Tradition and the State in Africa*, London, 1971, p. 13.
6   Richards, op. cit., p. 391.

To suggest that there appears little to be gained by thinking of African societies in terms of the concept of 'feudalism' implies a rejection neither of comparative work that includes European society, nor yet of the contribution the European medievalists can make to the study of African institutions[7].

But even so, methodologically, Goody expressed a certain preference:

But whereas Nadel and Maquet feel impelled to describe the societies they have studied as 'feudal', Smith, Fallers and Mair make at least as adequate an analysis without introducing the concept at all. This second approach seems preferable as a procedure. It is simpler; it minimizes the inevitable Western bias; and it helps to avoid the assumption that because we find vassalage (for example), we necessarily find the other institutions associated with it in medieval Europe. It is just these supposed interconnections which comparative study has to test rather than assume[8].

It is perhaps no accident that Goody's references are on this point specifically to anthropologists. As far as Africa is concerned, it had been mainly anthropologists who at all tried to make comparisons between African polities and those of feudal Europe. European medievalists had been inclined more towards the East than the South - the Middle East and most of Asia. This might have been out of ignorance about black Africa or out of considerations of comparability. Whatever the real reasons, in the British tradition it meant a fairly sharp dichotomy between historians and anthropologists. It entailed a certain lack, as British anthropologists were generally ahistorical. The same could have been said of the French school, if it had not been for the work of Suret-Canale. But, the basis of Suret-Canale's comparative analysis was the Asiatic mode of production rather than European feudalism. This is generally acknowledged, as is shown by the following statement by Coquery-Vidrovitch:

He (Suret-Canale) rediscovers the Asiatic mode of production in pre-colonial Black Africa at the culmination of a three-state development: from the 'primitive community' to the intermediary 'tribo-patriarchal' structures of the so-called 'archaic' or 'stateless' segmentary societies in which the fundamental unit is the extended

---

7   Goody, op. cit., p. 14.
8   Op. cit., p. 9.

family (lineage), ending with a well-differentiated class society in which, above the village patriarchy, there emerges a privileged aristocracy which determined the formation of the State[9].

Although in her remarks Coquery-Vidrovitch seem to be intent on controverting Suret-Canale, she nevertheless concedes that: "In its general conception this schema appears acceptable"[10]. But she refuses to credit it,

Since the structure and development of African pre-colonial societies was unique - in the first place fundamentally different from that of our Western societies[11].

If Suret-Canale's crime is to have extended the Asiatic mode of production to Africa, he cannot at the same time be accused of being unaware of the fundamental difference between African and Western societies. Furthermore, at this stage of our research, let alone fifteen years ago when the article in question was written, the uniqueness of African social structures cannot be a matter of assertion but rather of investigation. It is to our benefit that Suret-Canale short-circuited comparisons with European feudalism and broadened the scope for comparisons with other parts of the Third World. The debates that led almost to the rejection of the Asiatic mode of production as a theoretical construct did not significantly detract from his contribution. If the main issue had been resolved by replacing the Asiatic with a "tributary" mode of production, that might have entailed no substantive changes for Africa but first and foremost for the concept of "feudalism". The basic question still stands, irrespective of the demise of the Asiatic mode of production: does any generalized mode of production apply to pre-colonial Africa? Here the problem of uniqueness or variety versus generalization or unity (despite divergence of forms) asserts itself.

Although some writers such as Samir Amin make this appear to be purely a theoretical question, it is obvious that it is also empirical, especially in reference to Africa where our knowledge is still incomplete. If the latter were not the case, Meillassoux's work on Africa would not have assumed such great methodological and theoretical significance. Meillassoux's work, in contrast to Godelier's erudite digressions, capitalized on the specificity of the indigenous social formations in Africa. His essay[12] based

---

9   Coquery-Vidrovitch, C., in Seddon, (ed.) op. cit., p. 263.
10   Ibid.
11   Ibid.
12   Meillassoux, C., *The Economy in Agricultural Self-Sustaining Societies: A Preliminary Analysis*, 1978, (first published in French in 1960).

on the study of the Guro in the Ivory Coast, was a landmark for three reasons. Firstly, it used a Marxist methodology, without over-burdening the study with the orthodox lingua franca. Instead, it relied on the vernacular of kinship involving such terms as "lineage", "seniors", "juniors" and "matrimonial exchange". Secondly, from there on it attempted to formulate a general theory of the mode of production of self-sustaining pre-capitalist African societies or what later was unambiguously referred to as the "lineage mode of production" by Dupré and Rey[13]. Thirdly, it drew attention to a possible distinction between exchange which is a cause of production and exchange which is a result of production. In a direct and appreciative reference to Meillassoux's novel ideas, Coquery-Vidrovitch has this to say:

> In this respect Meillassoux's theoretical essay on the village self-sustaining community, innovatory in many ways, makes the transition from previous works of the French school, for it is a study of exchange, which is the most visible phenomenon, the immediate manifestation of the life of relationships. But he looks at exchange because it reflects the internal organization of the society, is the result of the organization of production and not its cause. He explains the absence of *exchange*, in the economic sense of the word, between members of the lineage community within the spheres of 'reciprocity', and 'redistribution', by the importance of kinship links ...[14].

Likewise, Dupré and Rey are appreciative of Meillassoux's revelations and are convinced that:

> Lineage society, by making explicit the fact that the place held by exchange - just like the place of exchange in capitalist society or place of the political in ancient Greek society - is to be explained by the role of exchange in the reproduction of the conditions of production, i.e. at a level other than that of exchange itself[15].

It is not as if these issues are free of controversy. In a later publication Samir Amin objected precisely to those theorists who "use the argument of variety of formations to negate the unifying principle (of the mode of production)" and declared that:

---

13   Dupré, G. and Rey, P.P., *Lineage Mode of Production*, 1968 in French and 1973 in English in Seddon.
14   Coquery-Vidrovitch, C., in Seddon (ed.), op. cit., p. 263.
15   Dupré, G., and Rey, P.P., in Seddon, op. cit., p. 188.

To the extent that I emphasize this conceptual distinction, I am rejecting arguments based on the variety of the immediate reality[16].

He further charged that, by refusing to make a radical distinction between relations of co-operation and domination and relations of exploitation, Meillassoux inevitably confuses the peasant mode of production and the domestic mode of production[17]. In an even more pointed attack on the French structuralist anthropologists Amin claims that:

> By demonstrating that the economic base is determinant in the last instance, some Marxist anthropologists have dispelled the confusion created by their structuralist colleagues, notably Maurice Godelier, in their attempt to treat kinship as part of the infrastructure and of the superstructure at the same time[18].

Although Meillassoux is included in the list of the approved anthropologists, Samir Amin is careful to point out that:

> I do not conclude from this that economic anthropology has thereby taught us how the dominance of the noneconomic realm functions in societies in the process of class formation, based on what Alain Marie calls the ideology of the family (or kinship)[19].

Consistent with this ambivalence towards anthropology and contrasting the dominance of local religions or kinship ideology in communal formations with the dominance of state religion in tributary formations, elsewhere Amin concludes that:

> This is why it is not anthropology but the history of great pre-capitalist societies which has the most to teach us about the dominance of the superstructure[20].

What about the "not-so-great" African pre-capitalist societies whose history is not given but whose existence is the starting point of a whole school of French Marxist anthropologists whose credentials in contemporary social theory are impeccable? It would seem that both Amin's conception of anthropology and the dividing line between forms of knowledge are surprisingly anachronistic. This is, perhaps, one of the points which our

---

16   Amin, S., op. cit., p. 50.
17   Op. cit., pp. 42-43.
18   Op. cit., p. 37
19   Ibid.
20   Op. cit., p. 52.

study of the interlacustrine social formations can illuminate. In fact, Samir Amin's series of hypotheses about the "tributary mode of production" will serve as a suitable testing ground.

Although some loose references to feudalism in Africa still persist in the literature, especially among leftists, serious research by a limited number of scholars mentioned earlier has shown that insistence on such analogies is patently unscientific. In the case of the interlacustrine kingdoms, as we have been at pains to point out, it would be a travesty of facts that can only lead to theoretical confusion. On the other hand, a search for an African mode of production such as have been proposed by Coquery-Vidrovitch might be a wild goose chase. Nor would the alternative be so attractive. A multiplicity of African modes of production would undoubtedly be a detraction from theory. But what theory? There are existing theories or historical categorisation which purport to be universal. Whatever our intellectual proclivities, they cannot be ignored. They can only be challenged by confronting them with new historical realities which up to now have been overlooked for political and ideological reasons. By a method of elimination, as we have done, or by radical transformation, we can hope to reach a more balanced view of human history in all its complexities.

In this regard, Samir Amin's work is important. He has proposed an outright elimination of the concepts of "feudalism" and "Asiatic mode of production", a process which is well under way in African studies. Procedurally, his method has been to collapse and assimilate them into what he offers as a more universal historical category, the "tributary mode of production". His reasons for this are that the two former concepts are, basically, ethnocentric. At this stage of our intellectual awareness nobody need quarrel with that supposition. What should be noted, however, is that the derivations of the "tributary mode of production", as advocated by Samir Amin, are negative. This is not to say that the connotations of the proposal are also negative. Unlike the Asiatic mode of production, Samir Amin's "tributary mode of production" has a substantive referent - a tributary relationship - which, theoretically, is capable of universalization. Whether it is or not is a question which Samir Amin alone cannot answer, except as a logical deduction based on certain glimpses of reality. For black Africa, which is an under-researched region historically, the proposed "tributary mode of production" must remain an hypothesis until more specific and systematic studies have been carried out in the region. In our view, this could best be done through sub-regional studies such as we have undertaken in the present work. Global studies not supported by concrete investigations might lose their theoretical and political relevance. This should have been self-evident, if it were not for the artificial but persistent dichotomy between particularity and universality or, even worse, the ill-conceived equation between specificity and the untheoretical.

Having rejected the "five-stage" theory, Samir Amin came up with his own "three-stage" theory - the communal, tributary and capitalist stage. He proclaims:

> Thus we have very general and abstract definitions of three forms of property - communal (of the land), tributary (of the land), capitalist (of means of production other than land[21]. These stress the content of property understood as social control, rather than its juridical and ideological forms[22].

Even though we have definite views on the first, it is the second mode of production with which we are concerned here. According to the above schema, the interlacustrine kingdoms can only be "tributary" and Samir Amin has treated the better known among them as such. Before any judgement can be passed on their inclusion, we have to know the basis for the classification. In a characteristic style Samir Amin has this laid out for us. According to him the following are the diagnostic features of the "tributary mode of production":

First, the surplus product is extracted by non-economic means by an exploiting class, as against a dominant group which does the same for purposes of collective use in the communal mode of production. Implicit in the latter is a rejection of Meillassoux's suggestion, and Dupré and Rey's, thesis that the elders in a lineage society constitute an exploiting class. On this point one cannot but agree with Samir Amin.

Second, the essential organization of production is based on use value and not on exchange value. This is a natural economy in which transfers, whatever their nature, do not represent commodity exchange. Samir Amin believes that the fault with a number of writers on feudalism is that they failed to make this distinction (e.g. Maurice Dobb, Kohachiro Takahashi, Rodney Hilton, etc.). To emphasize his point, he states that:

> Exchange in tributary formations is subject to the fundamental law of the tributary mode (i.e. use value) as land ownership is subject to the fundamental law of the capitalist mode in capitalist formations[23].

---

21   The grounds for excluding land as means of production in the capitalist form are not entirely clear.

22   Amin, op. cit., pp. 49-50.

23   Op. cit., p. 52.

Third, the tributary mode of production is characterized by the dominance of the superstructure. To prove his point, Samir Amin refers to the ideological role of the great religions such as Christianity, Islam, Hinduism, Buddhism and Confucianism in tributary social formations. He warns that:

> It is worth recalling that this domination aids in the extraction of the surplus, while the ideology of kinship in the communal mode, where ideology is also dominant, aids in the reproduction of relations of co-operation and domination but not of exploitation[24].

For that matter, Samir Amin sees state religion, as against local religions, as an essential feature of tributary social formations. Moreover, the class struggle is here muted by the dominance of the ideology of the ruling class.

Fourth, according to our author, one of the attributes of the tributary mode of production is "its appearance of stability and even of stagnation". This characteristic is supposed to be true of all tributary formations, including European feudalism, and is considered to be one of the consequences of the dominance of use value. Samir Amin, however, warns that this is only illusory and that:

> In fact, all tributary societies, whether in Egypt, China, Japan, India and South Asia, the Arabian and Persian East, North Africa and the Sudan, or Mediterranean or feudal Europe, have made great progress in the development of their productive forces[25].

Sub-Saharan Africa is conspicuous by its absence here. Perhaps, this is not accidental since elsewhere in response to Meillassoux's alleged scanty attention to the level of productive forces, Samir Amin remarks with some impatience that:

> Africanists too easily forget that the sub-Saharan societies they study had neither the plow nor a written language (except in Ethiopia and the Sudan)[26].

This point is critical to our study as well as to Samir Amin's definition of the "tributary mode of production". We return to it at the appropriate moment.

At this stage of our presentation it is sufficient merely to point out that in reference to any social formation "stability" or "stagnation" can hardly be

---

24   Ibid.
25   Op. cit., p. 54.
26   Op. cit., p. 42.

treated as definitional. This is more so that Samir Amin assures us that they are anyway only appearances even in the tributary mode of production. It transpires then that his real problem is to identify the dynamic forces in the tributary mode of production. One would have thought that increased demand for tribute would be the major force, underlying both class struggle and development of material forces. But in a rather incoherent passage, relying largely on analogies and metaphors, Amin thoroughly disabuses us when he declares:

> The search by the tributary class for a greater surplus is certainly not an inherent economic law analogous to the pursuit of capitalist profit[27].

But as a qualifying statement he says,

> ... it is the search for increased tribute - or even for the maintenance of tribute - which compels the tributary class, under the impetus of the peasant struggle, to improve production methods[28].

How so, if "the search for a greater surplus is certainly not an inherent economic law"? Elsewhere, after a short platitudinous statement about the role of production relations and in what strikes us as a moment of intellectual desperation, Amin comes up with the final clangor:

> However, the dynamic underlying the mechanism of development of the productive forces in the tributary mode lies in an area that simultaneously involves the base and the superstructure ... [29]. (The "area" is *unspecified*.)

This kind of fuzziness or imprecision would delight some of Samir Amin's antagonists such as Godelier who, at least, can point to the family structures which in their view straddles the terrain between the superstructure and the infrastructure. But, we know that Samir Amin's interest is in class and class-struggle, for he raises the following questions:

> How then is the class struggle carried out in the tributary mode and how does it necessarily lead to capitalism?[30]

27   Op. cit, p. 55. Cf Marx: "Where use-value predominates, no boundless, thirst for surplus labour arises from the nature of production", *Capital, Vol. 1*, p. 260.
28   Ibid.
29   Amin, S., op. cit., p. 54.
30   Ibid.

To this he gives another platitudinous answer:

> The class struggle between the peasant producers and their tributary
> exploiters spans the entire history of tributary formations ....[31].

After some gyrations and without a shred of evidence, he concludes:

> Nonetheless, the class struggle in the tributary mode is also the motive
> force of history because it is the contradiction that leads to the
> transcendence of this mode in accord with the objective necessities of
> the development of the productive forces[32].

How is this revealed, or are we to accept it as an article of faith? The
problem gets compounded when we are told in the same discourse that in
the tributary mode of production:

> The exploited class does not generally struggle for the total elimination
> of exploitation but only for its maintenance within the 'reasonable' limits
> necessary for the reproduction of economic life at a level of development
> of the productive forces where the surplus product is collectively used[33].

It would appear that the dominance of use value in pre-capitalist societies
has implications for both the development of productive forces and class
struggle which are profoundly different from those which are historically
associated with the capitalist mode of production. Although Samir Amin is
careful to state that:

> This difference ... prevents us from schematizing and mechanically
> transposing the functions and perspectives of the class struggle from the
> capitalist to the tributary mode ...[34],

The fact that he believes that each victory won by the peasants against
the exploiting tributary class favours "a third, nascent class, the bourgeoisie,
and thus opens the way to capitalism", casts doubt on his disclaimer. Why
is this necessarily the case? Is the European analogy asserting itself once
again here? Do we have evidence of the same in Egypt or of peasant
struggles at all against the Pharaohs? Or were the transformations that
occurred at a later stage attributable to other forces? It would seem that what
is necessary is the actual conditions for class struggle and not the outcome

---

31   Ibid.
32   Op. cit., p. 55.
33   Op. cit., p. 53.
34   Ibid.

of class struggles. The latter is contingent on a number of factors, including external ones, as modern history shows. If so, then there can only be a theory of the necessary material conditions for class struggle in different modes of production. For its construction a clear identification of the modes of production themselves is a necessary condition and, hence, our concern to discern more deeply the nature of African modes of production among others. This might lead to new discoveries or, at least, modification of classical definitions. In this respect Samir Amin's pioneering work on modes of production is highly pertinent.

Indeed, in the present work the interlacustrine kingdoms have been selected as candidates for Amin's "tributary mode of production". Mindful of the fact that abstract concepts do not stand in a one-to-one relationship with reality, we can benefit from applying his analytical scheme on them in an effort to separate the chaff from the grain. First, as was mentioned in Chapter V, the institution of *tribute* is found in all of them. This accords with Samir Amin's postulate about the extraction of surplus product by non-economic means in tributary formations. What might not be so self-evident is his otherwise valid distinction between an "exploiting class" and a "dominant group" such as are found in class and classless societies, respectively. While the association between office and extraction of tribute is not in doubt, what is not sure is whether or not the tribute beneficiaries in the interlacustrine kingdoms necessarily constituted a class. It seems to us that this issue cannot be clarified, without raising the question of property-relations and labour-relations which, according to theory, define modes of production. Samir Amin in his scheme has referred to tributary property in land[35] versus communal property. In our view, it is a serious misconception to talk of land as property in any sense of the word in African communal social formations south of the Sahara. There, the members of the community had only *use-rights* and land remained solely an instrument of labour. The significance of this observation becomes apparent when we consider what would have been "tributary property" in land in the interlacustrine kingdoms.

As will be recalled, in the pastoral kingdoms of Ankore, Rwanda and Burundi we found no evidence of property in land but rather administrative domains within which office-holders were entitled to collect tribute. Likewise, in the agricultural kingdoms of Buganda and Busoga the same principle prevailed. In Bunyoro, Toro, and Buhaya, although in theory the

---

35   In the actual text this appears as "tributary (of the land)", which could be read as "tributary property in land" or simply "fiefdoms".

same principle applied, there is evidence of office estates being gradually transformed into personal or private estates. Looking at the total situation, it could be argued that what we are witnessing here is societies in transition from non-property to property relations. The fact that consolidation of power in these polities went ahead and social reproduction stabilized over a period of up to four hundred years, without the development of property relations, would be no reason for not treating them as transitory. Lack of definite property-relations does not make them indistinguishable from communal social formations. This is not any more striking than the development of "capitalist agriculture" in most of sub-Saharan Africa without being necessarily accompanied by individual property rights in land. The same could be said of the development of industry under state capitalism. It is apparent that control over resources and labour can take forms other than property and that private appropriation of value is not contingent only on private property.

Conventionally, the second line of demarcation between modes of production is labour-relations. In the interlacustrine kingdoms, the labour process took three distinct forms simultaneously. First, there was family subsistence production which applied to all families, including that of the king for which his wives and domestic servants or slaves took responsibility. The main difference was that between the sexes. In agricultural production, with a few exceptions such as among the Bahutu, the women carried the major burden. In pastoralism animal husbandry was an exclusively male domain, but family herds were not tended necessarily by members of the family. They were often tended by clients or servants from families of humble background. This leads us directly to the second kind of labour process: namely, clientage. As had been reported earlier, patron-client relations were universal in the interlacustrine kingdoms. This was a personal and free contract whereby a man of wealth and high standing was offered personal services by a man of humble origins in exchange for mainly political protection and material support in times of need. In our view, the latter is relatively unimportant because from our study it is apparent that in the final analysis the labour of the client probably produced more value than he received. Not only did he work productively in the fields or among the herds of the patron for a number of days per week (a maximum of three in the interlacustrine), but also was obliged to give regular gifts to his patron and these usually took the form of produce during the season. Here, there was definitely extraction of economic value, *without expropriation or bondage.*

This would signal the importance of political domination over property relations. This is a ticklish point which is even better illustrated by the labour processes implicit in tributary relations. In all interlacustrine kingdoms office-holders treated their subordinates and those settled in their domains as vassals who owed them tribute which was shared with their superiors in ascending proportions. All over the interlacustrine area this took the form of perishable consumer goods, except cattle. Secondly, it did not involve any personal services. Perhaps, this was not necessary, since every office-holder had personal clients. In this respect all tribute-paying vassals were not labouring tenants even in Buganda where free access to land had been fore-closed by the king's suzerainty. Public service, including military services, was the only form of labour required of political dependents. In addition to labour-dues, commoners paid tribute which was a fixed portion of their produce. In some cases dues were imposed on such things as succession, marriage and burials. Tribute and dues are the third category of the labour process. What distinguishes them from the former two is that they were part of the fiscal policy of each kingdom and underwrote a higher standard of living among its office-bearers. But as most of the goods offered were perishable and the office-estates were in principle not heritable, the road to private accumulation was partially closed, except in the case of cattle. It is, therefore, reasonable to conclude that, while labour-relations in the strict sense were wanting among the interlacustrians, exploitation was general. This signified a movement away from relations of domination, which still persisted in truncated forms, to relations of exploitation, which nevertheless did not approach anything like Marx's concept of "generalized slavery".

We are here treading on treacherous ground, for we are trying to categorize what are otherwise processes of becoming. And yet, that is what is required in a definitional study such as ours. It is obvious that, unlike in lineage organization where juniors had an equal chance of becoming elders, in the interlacustrine kingdoms not every man had a chance of becoming an officer and an estate-holder. Secondly, once it had emerged, the governing bureaucracy was bound to look for mechanisms for perpetuating its domination. In the pastoral kingdoms monopoly over cattle was one way of effecting this. As is shown by the case of Bunyoro and Buhaya, estate-holders were also looking for opportunities to pass down official estates to their heirs. But this practice was not at all general in any of the kingdoms. This somewhat detracts from Samir Amin's first postulate because those who were responsible for the extraction of tribute were not identifiable in terms of their relation either to property or to labour. In the absence of property-relations or definite labour-relations we cannot conclude, as a matter of fact, that the tribute-recepients in the interlacustrine kingdoms constituted an "exploiting class". They were exploiters alright;

but of what sort is the question that must be answered scientifically, and not ideologically. Meantime, we note that their biggest asset was *political control*, whose lack of establishment nonetheless makes it difficult for us to regard it as class-property in the conventional sense.

Samir Amin's second postulate, that in tributary formations "the essential organization of production is based on use value and not exchange" and that in these societies "exchange ... is subject to the fundamental law of the tributary mode", namely, use-value, is fully confirmed. As was mentioned earlier, production and all trade, local as well as long-distance, was totally dominated by use-value in the interlacustrine social formations. Consequently, no merchant capital of any sort emerged in the region. But then what of the supposed "dissolving effect" of long-distance trade on pre-capitalist formations which had been stressed by so many Marxist writers, including Samir Amin and Coquery-Vidrovitch? Although Coquery-Vidrovitch concedes that, "founded upon war and trade, production is sterile"[36], she is nonetheless convinced that long-distance trade played a decisive role in the consolidation of the state in tropical Africa. This is not true of the interlacustrine kingdoms. Not only were they fully formed long before trade started, but that the majority of them, especially the pastoral ones, were never involved in trade (as against barter) until the colonial era. It seems that real productive forces can only be internal to an economy, seeing that participation by kingdoms such as Buganda, Bunyoro and Buzinza in long-distance trade in the 19th century did not bring about any appreciable difference in their level of development of the material forces as compared to the other kingdoms in the region. This does not in itself disprove circulationist theories in general, but it does cast doubt on them.

The third postulate advanced by Samir Amin is that the tributary mode of production is characterized by the dominance of the superstructure. In support of his point of view, he invokes the great religions of the East and Christianity, which facilitated the "extraction of the surplus" and cemented relations of exploitation. Accordingly, he presents state religion as an essential feature of tributary formations. There can be no doubt that the superstructure was particularly dominant in the interlacustrine kingdoms. What is not clear is whether or not there were state religions. The question is whether kingship rituals and ceremonies such as the new moon ceremonies and dairy rituals; the jaw-bone oracles and Lubale cults in

---

36   Op. cit., p. 284.

Buganda, all of which did not refer to the rest of the population but rather to the super-human attributes of the king, should be regarded as state religions. The problem is compounded by the fact ancestor-cult prevailed at all levels in these societies. As will be remembered, kinship ideology is supposed to aid the reproduction of relations of domination and not of exploitation. We are inclined to think that in the interlacustrine kingdoms there was no clear separation between the two, even though the principle of kinship had been largely superseded. This harks back to the question of political domination versus class exploitation or labour-relations. Suffice it to say here that the interlacustrine kingdoms fall short of Samir Amin's criterion of religion. Although this might appear as an empiricist or static view, there are theoretical reasons for it which will be adduced in the next chapter.

We have already rejected Samir Amin's fourth postulate about "stagnation" or "stability" on theoretical and logical grounds. This is not to say that in particular instances societies cannot be described in these terms, but that such descriptions cannot be offered as theoretical categories. For instance, any argument that the interlacustrine kingdoms were stagnant by virtue of their mode of production would be very difficult to sustain. Relative differences are discernible among them. Whereas the predominantly pastoral formations such as Ankore, Rwanda and Burundi showed signs of stagnation and a certain amount of decadence among their "divine" kings, the predominantly agricultural formations such as Buganda, Busoga, Buhaya and Buha exhibited great political dynamism. In them office-holders were jogging for positions and the rulers were determined to smash the remnants of kinship organisation. However, in the economic sphere their zeal was less striking. In other words, they mobilized the "peasants" more for political and military purposes than for production. If it were not for the case of Bunyoro which also had a pastoral kingship, it would have been easy to reduce the whole issue to a distinction between pastoralism and arable agriculture. Nevertheless, even Bunyoro could not fully suffice as a basis for a counter-argument against such a procedure since, after the loss of their herds[37], its rulers came to depend more and more on agriculture and landed estates for their sustenance.

The distinction between these two forms of subsistence is worth pursuing for two main reasons. First, purely pastoral economies, as was remarked in Chapter 2, have not in history been associated with a high level of development of material forces. Even as instruments of labour, the fact that

---

37   cf Beattie, op. cit. p. 1.

cattle are consumed directly might be of theoretical significance. This is in contrast to land which cannot be so consumed except through cultivation of a great variety of crops, as was the case in the agricultural kingdoms. Secondly, when capitalism was introduced in the interlacustrine region, the pastoral elites were totally eclipsed, whereas the agricultural ones flourished more than ever before. It is arguable that the insistence by pastoralists on antiquated forms of production is what could, objectively, be referred to as stagnation. *Antiquated* is the operative word here and not simply continuance of a mode of production over a very long period of time. In other words, we might have to ponder the question as to when a mode of production is antiquated or outmoded, so to speak, before we decide whether or not it is stagnant.

Coquery-Vidrovitch's treatment of this specific topic must be regarded as an improvement on Samir Amin's sweeping generalization about "stagnation". In her well-known article, "Research on an African Mode of Production", she makes the following observation:

> In reality, it seems that this type of speculation (why Africa did not develop) is a bad start; it reduces technology to being the driving force of the stagnation development alternative. But the weak level of the productive forces, though it is the most obvious sign of stagnation, is not necessarily its cause. In Black Africa there has always been a potential agricultural surplus. The reason why it was not exploited was perhaps less the determinism of the natural environment or the ignorance of man, than it was an economic choice resulting from all the social components[38].

The idea of *economic choice* is most suggestive. It effectively dispenses with the usual stereo-type arguments about ignorance. All evidence indicates that Africans knew about the plough and the wheel, and yet they did not adopt it. Why? As Coquery-Vidrovitch suggests, the structure of demand must have something to do with it. It is, indeed, a perverse capitalist idea that human beings have a natural urge to accumulate for the sake of accumulation or would go out of their way to adopt new techniques for the sake of progress (where to?) in their respective societies. Could not they be satisfied with what they have and, consequently, confine their energies to the maintenance of existing stocks? Would not this be the major implication of the dominance of use-value? In answering these questions, it must be noted that maintenance of existing stocks need not be viewed statically, as

---

38   Seddon, op. cit., p. 264.

the demand for goods or level of production could fluctuate according to changing social and physical conditions.

In the interlacustrine kingdoms the supply of both pastoral and agricultural products remained fairly adequate and unvaried. Nature's bounty was such that the Nganda cows yielded enough to satisfy the needs of the milk and butter consuming Batutsi and Bahima overlords; so did the banana groves to meet the consumption needs of all and sundry. The situation prevailed until the middle of the 19th century, if not later. Even long-distance trade with Zanzibar did not have any dissolving effect. Although over-generalized, the thrust of Coquery-Vidrovitch's argument coincides with our observation. This is how she summarizes her point of view:

> It seems to us that one of the driving forces in the history of the people of Black Africa is to be found in the dialectical interplay of the relations ... between apparently heterogeneous socioeconomic levels within the same totality (the co-existence of community clan structures with the territorial system and the superimposition of family self-sufficiency and long distance trade); at each moment this force corresponds to a certain stage in the development of the relations governing these elements, which are contradictory and therefore persistently generate disequilibrium and conflict[39].

This is what she refers to as the "African mode of production" and resists any attempt to subsume it under the Asiatic mode of production (or a modified version thereof) because:

> The only thing shared by these two systems is the existence of self-sustaining village communities. But the former (Asiatic mode) has despotism and direct exploitation through general slavery; and in the latter (African mode) ... the superimposed bureaucracy only interfered indirectly in the community. We do not see the need, one which disregards accuracy, to include two types of production which differ in so many respects in the same framework[40].

Her final objection, which provides a counter-point to Samir Amin's ceaseless quest in the "tributary mode of production", is that:

---

39   Seddon, op. cit., p. 276.
40   Ibid.

However, it seems excessive to look for the driving force of the development of African societies *only* in the contribution of the productive forces of self-sufficiency. This assertion, as an attempt to rediscover the pair 'exploiters/exploited' within the self-enclosed African society, reveals a lack of observation of the real facts ...[41].

It is worth reiterating here that insistence on real facts or concrete studies is inspired by a desire to establish well-founded generalizations. Her search for a single African mode of production is as contrary to her prescription as Samir Amin's attempt to universalize all the attributes of the "tributary mode of production" from the rest of the world to Africa. For instance, her comparison between the west African kingdoms and the Zulu kingdom in Southern Africa is as much a violation of facts as is Samir Amin's comparison between the great religions of the East and the pre-Islamic religions in some sub-Saharan kingdoms. For that matter, one suspects that even a comparison between the post-Islamic kingdoms in West Africa and the kingdoms in East, Central and Southern Africa might hide certain basic differences. For example, in West Africa trade was more general, the processes of accumulation more advanced and the class relations more crystallized than anywhere else in black Africa. Labour-relations in West Africa included slavery which violated all kinship or quasi-kinship relations of domination and transformed them into relations of class exploitation, without any question. This should serve as a warning against Coquery-Vidrovitch's general belief about the co-existence between "clan structures" and "family self-sufficient" communities and "superimposed" territorial systems or bureaucracies in Africa. Not all black Africa fits this description, important as it is.

Therefore, the search for the pair, "exploiter"/"exploited" in some parts of black Africa is not in vain. However, the question is: was slavery and long-distance trade the "dissolving factor" in all the great kingdoms of west Africa? The Mossi kingdoms have been used by writers such as Suret-Canale to prove that long-distance trade was not a necessary condition for the rise of kingdoms in Africa. This is probably true of many more kingdoms in black Africa, as is shown by the interlacustrine States. What remains is the question of slavery. The Mossi kings were avid slave-raiders. Did this dissolve kinship relations and transform local relations of domination into relations of exploitation? If yes, then we have a problem since neither long-distance trade nor slavery would be a necessary factor in

---

41   Ibid.

the development of a great many African kingdoms. Even in West Africa it does not seem that class exploitation was based on landed property nor did it entail universal elimination of control over land by lineage groups and the destruction of the household economy among free citizens. The point we are driving at here is that, bearing in mind all the differences between the various regions in Africa, can it be assumed that contradictions within the tributary mode of production in Africa could have been solved only by the development of private property in land, as in Europe? Could it then be concluded that the persistence of kinship and the household economy in the interlacustrine kingdoms was a transient phenomenon?

In his studies on Africa, G. Balandier had always been impressed by the interplay between lineage and the state in African politics. He saw this as characteristic. Coquery-Vidrovitch, probably under his influence, went further and perceived this as a source of "disequilibrium and conflict", if we recall. In Buganda where the clans had been deprived of all their land rights, open conflict between the *Kabaka* and the clan leaders occurred and led to a state of disequilibrium for nearly fifty years. Elsewhere in the interlacustrine area, centralizing monarchs accommodated clan and lineage groups by allowing them effective occupation of the land, while subordinating them to the demands of a territorial bureaucracy. In other words, these monarchs found another way of achieving the same objectives as the kings of Buganda. This calls to mind one of Godelier's earlier suggestion that there can be another path and another form for the mode of production, by which a minority dominates and exploits the community without directly interfering with the conditions of production but by profitably taking a surplus in labour and in products[42]. The conflict of interests remains, but there is no reason why it should lead to disequilibrium, if the land is abundant and the demands on the producers are not onerous. This is what seems to have obtained in all the interlacustrine kingdoms up to the middle of the 19th century.

The regional variations alluded to above can support more than one thesis. At the same time they are an important reminder that Africa is a big and unevenly developed continent. It is only through systematic regional studies, which brook no distinction between social anthropological and economic historical development, that we can hope to establish the necessary rules of exclusion, without relativising theory.

---

42   Godelier, M., *Perspectives in Marxist Anthropology*, Cambridge, 1977 (first published in French in 1973).

In other words, the insistence on regional specificity should not be confused with a desire to build taxonomic categories which are capable of only empiricist statements. The main point is that in generalizing we should be sufficiently alert to differences in quality, to perceive opportunities for generating new concepts or theories. For instance, the apparent conflict between territorial and lineage organization in sub-Saharan Africa can be clarified by a careful comparison between the savannah kingdoms of West Africa, where Islam and slavery became pervasive factors, and other kingdoms in which development was more autonomous, such as in the interlacustrine region. This can be done without assuming any unilineal growth among African kingdoms, irrespective of major intervening variables. Likewise, comparisons between tributary social formations in Africa and in other regions can be conducted, without assuming that the appearance of the tributary relation signals the disappearance of the household economy and usufructuary rights in land in Africa in favour of generalized slavery. Equally important, would be a comparative analysis of African conceptions of "property rights", without assuming that all is destined towards the bourgeois or capitalist concept of property. In the next chapter the intention is to arrive at a categorisation of the interlacustrine kingdoms, while taking into account the various mediations just mentioned. The implicit notion is that these recur in so many African social formations that they merit rethinking.

RETHINKING MODES OF PRODUCTION IN AFRICA

Rethinking modes of production in Africa might sound glamorous and even pretentious, but behind this is a serious concern and even a painful struggle to understand the present as history. In this case the subject-object is African history, not merely in itself but as part of universal history. As the last four chapters have shown, this gives rise to terminological and conceptual problems. Uncharitably interpreted, this could be seen as a product of a confused mind. But, fundamentally, what is at stake is the desire to comprehend world history in a generative way and not in a reductionist way, as often happens. This inevitably draws our attention to the specificity of historical instances. But, as is known, history is deciphered differently in different epochs. In this context our appeal for rethinking modes of production in Africa is fully justified. However, as any radical scholar would know, this often leads to unconventional usage of terms and concepts which might become a source of confusion or controversy. Our constant struggle with terms and concepts in the last four chapters bears witness to this. Consequently, the intention in this chapter is to resolve some of the apparent terminological and conceptual inconsistencies.

The first term we have subjected to critical reexamination is "tribe". This had already been fore-shadowed in an earlier study, "The Ideology of Tribalism"[1]. This work was a reaction to the abuse of the term, "tribe", in African studies and the frequent temptation to reduce apparent contradictions among modern Africans to "tribalism". Despite the persistence of this tendency in the mass media, the rediscovery of "tribalism" in Africa by some late-comers such as the Latin Americans and some reservations among empiricists, there is a general consensus among African scholars and other Africanists that "tribalism" is more an ideological reflex than an index of some concrete existence in Africa. It is regrettable that our earlier postulate had been taken by some to mean a complete denial of the existence of tribes in Africa. Yet, the kernel of our argument in the original article, as in the present work, was that the idea that all African societies were "tribes" was a result of the colonial legacy on the continent. Unlike

---

1   See Mafeje, A., *The Ideology of Tribalism*, JMAS, 9, 2 (1971) pp. 253-61.

the present work, the original paper was not definitional and was concerned mainly with exposing the falsity of that assumption by pointing to contrary cases.

In the present work refutations have taken a more positive form i.e. the attempt to distinguish between different forms of social organization is premised on a careful identification of various social formations. Indeed, one of the main arguments in the study is that what had been categorised as "tribes" in the interlacustrine region is on close inspection a mixture of tribes and kingdoms at different stages of becoming. It is further argued that the actors in the various stages are one and the same peoples. In that sense the term "tribe" does not refer to people but rather to a particular form of political and social organization. We are careful here, as in the general text, not to include economic organization. The main reason for this is that although, conventionally, we are used to talking about "tribal economy", this is a misconception since historically-known African tribes were characterized by lack of economic integration at the tribal level. Household economy was their general feature.

Empirically, we know of only family herds and fields. This is in sharp contrast to the Asian village economies or the tendency towards economic integration in tributary social formations. In contemporary Africa where social formations are generally balkanized and combined unevenly, this might be an important consideration. Theoretically, it is not without significance that both bourgeois and Marxist economists have referred to tribal societies as societies without an *economic system*. The same conclusion could be drawn from Meillassoux's theory of the *lineage* mode of production and would emphasize the absence of classes in this type of societies which are segmentary or marked by vertical cleavages. Consequently, what is communal in the context of household economy is the right of access, not of property or value outside the lineage. In such a system, prestations to the chief, we argued, are an affirmation of a political rather than an economic relation.

The absence of any recognizable property-relations in land in traditional African societies is probably the hardest point to assimilate into classical European theories - Marxist and non-Marxist. This has led to a number of misconceptions and actual distortions, if only for the sake of explaining the same social phenomena as are found elsewhere in the world. In Europe, especially, these took the form of class and property. Regarding the latter, it is easy to show that in its juridical sense the concept is inapplicable to most of black Africa. As we have seen in the case of the interlacustrine societies, *use-rights* deriving from community membership were the over-riding principle. This does not shift the burden of ownership, as is often supposed, to the community. The idea of "communal ownership" of land is still a result of a particular fixation with "property".

The traditional African community did not conceive of land in terms of ownership but in terms of *dominum eminens* within which use-rights were guaranteed. These were activated through family units and could get entrenched, depending on demographic pressure and the use to which different types of soil were put. The fact that individual families were units of production as well as of appropriation and could hold their plots of land in perpetuity as long as they were under use casts doubt on the supposition by liberal economists and Marxists alike that the so-called communal land tenure necessarily militated against the development of material forces in Africa. It is important to note that capitalist production has occurred in black Africa since the introduction of cash crops, without any significant changes in land tenure systems but more in land use. We are also reminded of the fact that in the orient production increased and great technological innovations occurred over a very long time, without the development of individual property rights. The same is true of the great, pre-Columbian empires of Latin America. In the light of all this, individual property rights, as a necessary condition for development, must remain an attribute of European natural theology.

It would be foolish to conclude from the foregoing discussion that absence of property-rights in traditional African societies meant absence of exploitation and domination. As is illustrated by the interlacustrine societies, nothing would be farther from the truth. The problem, however, is how to conceive of the processes of exploitation and domination in this type of society. Writers such as Samir Amin have made a distinction between relations of domination and relations of exploitation. This distinction hinges not so much on social inequalities as on the presence or absence of class relations. According to this view, tribal or communal social formations are marked, instead of classes, by kinship hierarchies which nonetheless have a redistributive function. Hence, in this case domination is not necessarily correlated with exploitation. This has been contested by writers such as Rey and Dupré, who believe that women and juniors were exploited by the elders who, by virtue of this, constituted a class. However, as has been pointed out, their thesis is undermined by the fact that elders are not owners but merely custodians of a patrimony/matrimony and are under a kinship obligation to surrender power to their juniors when the time comes. Certainly, this would not apply to classes.

Nevertheless, two main issues arise from this. First, the question is whether exploitation *per se* implies necessarily existence of classes in a society. Secondly, is the existence of classes in any society contingent on property-relations? Evidence from the interlacustrine region and from elsewhere would indicate that exploitation is quite possible, without the existence of distinct classes. Some dogmatic or crude Marxists find it difficult to credit this because for them "class-analysis" marks the beginning and the end of dialectical and historical materialism. Yet, the exploitation of such social categories as women, juniors and ethnic groups is amenable to a materialist interpretation, without denying such categories their particular identity. This is more so when we deal with what has been described as "pre-capitalist societies". Out of prejudice or dogmatism, these societies have been treated as out of the purview of dialectical materialism and as relics of the past - stuff suitable for anthropological foibles. Indeed, it is the virtue of the French school of anthropologists to have demonstrated that dialectical materialism as an epistemology is not limited only to class societies. However, the problem is that the analytical categories associated with historical materialism presuppose the existence of classes. The resurrection of political economy, which Marx had denounced in no uncertain terms, in development studies points to a felt-need to comprehend the totality of human existence beyond the confines of modern European history. Inevitably, this calls, for a serious revision of designating categories. Some of these may be found in antiquity and some might have to be found *de novo* i.e. anew.

In the preceding chapters we reached the conclusion that in the interlacustrine kingdoms there was general exploitation of the ordinary citizens, but we could not decide whether or not this meant class exploitation in all cases. The main reason was general lack of property-relations in land, the most important asset in agrarian societies. The second reason was the undeveloped state of labour-relations. Tenants and clients got exploited by virtue of their political subordination and not so much as labour. Their exploitation took the form of tribute and public services. Personal services were very limited. This led us to the conclusion that exploitation in the interlacustrine kingdoms was through extra-economic means. This deprived us of the two basic criteria, property- and labour-relations, which determined class-relations in classical European societies. What we were left with was superordinate and subordinate categories which could reproduce themselves only by political and ideological means. Ownership of large herds of cattle in the pastoral kingdoms and retention of what was otherwise official estates through descending generations in Buhaya and Bunyoro was still very much a function of political status.

Let it be admitted from the onset that "status" is a non-Marxist concept. It received its most systematic treatment from Max Weber, who happens to have been one of Marx's foremost antagonists. This in itself does not deprive the concept of any substantive referent. The epistemological problem is, however, that Weber's critique of Marx was conducted from a strictly idealist standpoint. Therefore, any adoption of his concepts is liable to accusations of eclecticism. And yet, Weber acknowledged the importance of classes in modern societies but was concerned substantively to distinguish between "class-structured" societies in which goods and services were distributed through "property" and "market relations" and "status-group-structured" societies in which goods and services were distributed according to "rank" or "prestige". Accordingly, for him "class" and "status-group" *ständ* were opposed categories and, historically, represented the dividing-line between traditional patrimonial and modern capitalist society. In the absence of any clear Marxist concepts for dealing with pre-capitalist societies, Weber's retreat was logically justified. Furthermore, it is not any worse than the retreat into the language of political economy in development studies or the return to circulationist arguments by French Marxist anthropologists in dealing with lineage societies.

An advance on this position would be to contemplate, despite Marx, the question of whether in future developments the economic factor will continue to be in command, as against the political-ideological factor (Weber's moral-cultural order). In other words, if capitalism is inevitable how do we explain the revulsions against it in some parts of the Third World? What are the appropriate Marxist concepts for analyzing such phenomena as nationalism and religious revivalism in these countries? The fusion of pre-capitalist and capitalist elements in these societies makes it imperative for us to look for new concepts or to adapt old ones. For instance, it is apparent from the study of the interlacustrine and other African societies that class-relations cannot be limited only to property-relations. Nor could exploitation be restricted only to labour-relations. Political and ideological control can be just as effective under certain conditions. These would include state capitalism, bureaucratic socialism and the so-called managerial "class" in advanced capitalist societies. But for the time being, our immediate task is to contend with the theoretical problems which arise from the study of the interlacustrine kingdoms.

The interlacustrine kingdoms have been described as "tribal", "multi-tribal" (divisible into a number of "ethnic" groups) and "feudal". Only the last term has class connotations. The general belief was that the Bahuma in Bunyoro, the Bahima in Ankore, the Batutsi in Rwanda and Burundi, and the Bahaya in Bukoba constituted "feudal aristocracies". But, as has been shown in Chapters IV and V, these kingdoms exhibited none of the features which had been characteristic of feudalism in Europe. It seemed, therefore, it would be sheer nonsense to persist in calling them "feudal". As is illustrated by our earlier references, there is a growing body of opinion to the same effect. Among these Samir Amin has the distinction of having put forward a clear alternative theoretical construct, namely, the *tributary mode of production*. In the context of the interlacustrine kingdoms this is extremely suggestive, since the principle of tribute is pervasive among them. This was one of our principal grounds for rejecting the anthropological idea that the interlacustrine kingdoms were "tribes". From the available evidence, it could be demonstrated that tribute, among other things, made the rise of a non-producing bureaucracy possible. This had far-reaching implications. Among these was the question of ethnicity and class. Our approach to the problem was to posit that in general ethnography has nothing to do with racial or ethnic origins but more with the generation of social meanings and systems of social classification in particular historical contexts. It was argued that we know this to be the case because the same people over time can and often produce different ethnographies. Likewise, peoples of different origins living side by side can and often do become authors of the same ethnographies. It was strongly argued in the relevant chapters that such distinctions as are made in the interlacustrine region between Bairu/Bahuma, Bairu/Bahinda, Batutsi/Bahutu were not natural but social systems of classification. We contended that it was an anthropological fallacy to suppose that there could be a single tribe called "Bairu" which was spread all over the interlacustrine region. Sociologically, it makes more sense to accept the fact that the "Bairu" in Bunyoro, Ankore, Buhaya, Buha and Buzinza are first and foremost Banyoro, BanyAnkore, Bahaya, Baha and Bazinza respectively and only secondarily "Bairu". This is so because an elevated "Muiru" ceases to be one, socially, in all the kingdoms mentioned. Likewise, as witnessed in Buhaya, Buha, Buzinza, Rwanda and Burundi, degraded or non-royal Bahinda and Batutsi got assimilated into intermediate categories referred to by different names such as Batare, Bezi, Bataga, etc. in Burundi or "Nfura" in Buhaya and the neighbouring kingdoms. In addition, the process of social elevation and degradation of certain categories of people facilitated intermarriage among members of a category, irrespective of their actual origins. This makes it difficult to talk about caste in any serious sense in these circumstances.

In describing the processes of social mobility and social differentiation referred to above, we have refrained from using the concept of "class" immediately. Instead, we have adhered to the concept of "status-category". This is not an evasion, as some impatient Marxists might think. It is in an effort to avoid unnecessary distortions so as to see more clearly what the realities of the African situation are before we commit ourselves. While it is true that the movement up and down the social scale in the interlacustrine kingdoms was correlated with privilege or lack of privilege, it would be a mistake to suppose that this could be construed immediately in terms of property. It is well to remember that the allocation of value in these societies was strictly extra-economic i.e. political and ideological. Furthermore, the value so allocated was in all cases *use value* beyond which any differences were merely in quantity and not in quality. In other words, the higher the rank, the greater the access to the same utilities. The king of Rwanda might have had greater access to butter and milk, and banana-beer but he consumed so much and no more. In fact, the abstemiousness of the Batutsi kings and their almost supercilious contempt for gluttony might have affected the potential demand for utilities. This might be an extreme example, but the general evidence from the interlacustrine is that the rulers in this region were not over-demanding economically. In contrast to what happened in the orient, there was hardly any pressure on the producers in the interlacustrine to intensify production. In turn, this might account for the slow technological progress in the region. In this regard, Samir Amin's assertion that increased demand for tribute and utilities cannot be offered as an explanation for technological innovations in tributary societies has to be treated as an unwarranted supposition. One suspects that the splendour of ancient Egypt, Mesopotamia, Japan, China, Bali, Java and Thailand reflected not only increased extraction of value from the producers but also intensification of production and technological factors in which the state played an important role. Under these conditions rank got associated with a different style of life and material well-being. Those who were in charge of the system were thus able to reproduce themselves socially in a sustained way and ultimately formed a distinct class.

In contrast, in the interlacustrine the household economy prevailed. The members of the bureaucracy, no less than ordinary citizens, depended largely on their families for subsistence. The surplus they received in the form of tribute either as patrons in their own right or as clients of the king was neither convertible into luxury goods nor durable, except cattle perhaps. These two factors reduced the prospects for developing a distinct life-style which continued, irrespective of individual political fortunes. On losing his rank, a Muganda chief reverted to the status of peasant *mukopi*[2]. Similarly, on losing his herds, a Mututsi or Muhima man of rank, had nothing else to show and fell into oblivion. On the other hand, a Muhutu or Muiru who somehow acquired large herds of cattle came into political and social prominence. All

---

2   In Luganda *mukopi* is not an occupational term but rather a status term - a person of no special social standing.

this would indicate the fragility of the economic base which was essentially undergirded by the household economy and the weaknesses of a bureaucracy which still worked through individuals in the absence of a formed class, capable of reproducing itself indefinitely. In Buhaya and Bunyoro there might have been the beginnings of the latter due to a growing hold on landed property by some chiefly families.

This notwithstanding, the general argument in the preceding paragraph brings us back to the use of the term, "status-category", in preference to other terms in dealing with the social character of the interlacustrine kingdoms. As has been mentioned, Weber used the term, "status-group" to refer to those who occupied more or less the same social rank and enjoyed the same social prestige in patrimonial societies. Weber's "patrimonial society" could not have included feudalism because value was allocated according to rank and prestige, for example chiefs versus commoners or "Bairu" versus Bahima, it is important to point out that in their case this was not a group phenomenon. It was rather a matter of large social categories of people who did not necessarily interact with one another and whose individual positions and group membership varied widely. For instance, "Bairu" referred to a residual category of non-pastoralists who could be anything from an ordinary cultivator, a client, to a servant. Those of them who acquired cattle fell into a different category and enjoyed more or less the same privileges as the pastoralists, including eligibility for official posts and marriage into a superior category. In the event their social status and categorisation changed as instanced by the term *nfura* in Buhaya or *banyaruguru* in Burundi. In the opposite direction, fallen Bahinda and Batutsi in Buhaya, Buha and Buzinza got re-categorized in such a way that they became undistinguishable from some of the Bairu and even practised agriculture. In Burundi those Bahinda who were not royalty (not descendants of Mututsi) were accorded a different "tribal" name. In our view, this dispels any illusions about ethnicity being a defining social category.

On the other hand, there has been a great temptation on the part of the radical left in East Africa to put "class" labels *a priori* on the processes of differentiation we have just described. For instance, the "Bairu" have been presented *en bloc* as an exploited "peasant class", the Bahima or Batutsi as an exploiting "feudal aristocracy" and so and so on. From our analysis it is apparent that not only were these amorphous categories but were also fairly fluid. Within them and across them, individuals and groups were constantly changing positions. We have the supreme example of Buganda where the so-called peasants *bakopi* were interchangeable with chiefs during the 19th century. At this point in time even boundaries between kingdoms were extremely fluid. It was British and Belgian colonialism which put an end to this dynamism and sought to confer a permanent status on the existing social categories. The ruling monarchs and their staff were seen through feudal lenses and were confirmed as such. Small kingdoms were reduced to chiefdoms, recalcitrant powerful kings such as Kabarega of Bunyoro were deposed and replaced with pliant monarchs who accepted the dictates of the colonial government. Traditional tribute was converted into taxes to raise revenues from which the surviving kings and staff could be paid. In some cases such as Buganda the original administrative domains held by chiefs were allotted to them as private estates. Thus, property-relations were created where none existed before. Likewise, royal estates, as against *dominum eminens*, got privatized.

It is easy to project from this backwards and impute the existence of feudalism in the interlacustrine kingdoms before colonialism. Yet, if the distortions of colonial capitalism are to be fully appreciated and overcome, a deeper understanding of pre-colonial African formations is necessary. Also, the theoretical desire to bring to bear specifically African perspectives on what has been paraded as universal history is not unwarranted. For instance, the interlacustrine kingdoms could be described as "tributary formations". But that could easily degenerate into a parody, if sufficient care is not taken to overcome certain incompatibilities with or conceptual inadequacies in existing theories. Our insistence on the prevalence of status-categories in the interlacustrine kingdoms serves two purposes. First, it shows that these societies were one step removed from tribal or segmentary societies in which status-categories were kinship-bound. In the interlacustrine kingdoms these had got considerably expanded to embrace whole "tribes" within what was objectively one social formation. Conceptually, the existence of tribes within a non-tribal social formation in the strict sense constituted an anomaly, a contradiction in terms. Recognition of the historically-founded fact that here the term, "tribe", was used as a metaphor for something else obviated the apparent contradiction. Secondly, the discovery of non-tribal status-categories paved the way for further enquiry into their exact nature and probable predispositions.

First of all, while, like all status-categories they are ideologically derived, unlike tribal categories, they are not prescriptive. As we have seen, they allow political as well as economic mobility. Individuals, irrespective of their categorisation, could achieve eminence or suffer degradation as was shown. The critical difference between this and a class-society is that, promotion depended less on property than on *service*. In these societies virtually every adult male was somebody's client and loyal clients were rewarded, materially and politically. Throughout the interlacustrine kingdoms, *patron-client* relations had become the primary means for political action. Indeed, it is our hypothesis that with the passing of tribal society, patron-client relations gradually replaced kinship politics. In sharp contrast to kinship relations, however, they were strictly dyadic and voluntary, and allowed exploitation and individual self-aggrandizement. Patrons disposed of the services of their clients as they pleased and could lay claim on the possessions of their clients at will. On their part, clients would tolerate all this as long as they saw opportunities for self-aggrandizement, which often meant getting into a position where they became patrons in their own right. This gave rise to a hierarchy of dyadic relations up to the king himself. In other words, these relations traversed as well as straddled given status-categories. A Muhima could be a client of another Muhima in the same way as Bairu were often clients of Bahima; or a chief could be a client of another chief in the same way as commoners were often clients of particular chiefs.

Having clarified the shift from kinship to patron-client relations and having identified the locus of political power in the interlacustrine kingdoms, we now propose to relate all this to the economic instance so as to arrive at a proper characterization of the whole social formation. We have already emphasized the general lack of property-relations in the interlacustrine kingdoms. We did so, without denying the existence of exploitative relations in the region. "Exploitation", as a term, has very strong ideological connotations, so much so that liberals recoil from it with embarrassment. On the other hand, Marxists often use it as an ideological weapon to beat down their embarrassed adversaries. Some get caught up in a logical contradiction here because while, on the one hand, they might denounce it morally, on the other hand, they might theoretically see it as a necessary condition for development. As a result of the latter, a number of Marxists go out of their way to find "classes" even where none exist. While not guilty of the same crime, writers such as Samir Amin who see lack of property-relations in African communal systems as a hindrance to development and who, conversely, see capitalism as a necessary state for the intensification of technological factors could be accused of making a virtue of what they otherwise reject ideologically. Of course, exploitation need not be equated with class any more than productive use of economic surplus is correlated with class.

In the interlacustrine kingdoms exploitation assumed the form of tribute and services. In the first instance, tribute was paid to the state by all subjects who were otherwise freemen and autonomous producers. This passed through a hierarchy of state officials, starting from the local level up to the royal palace. Each of the officials was entitled to a fixed share of the tribute. In addition, all citizens were liable to *public* services such as military services, construction of roads and bridges, and maintenance of official dwellings, including royal palaces which were nothing else but a grander version of the same perishable huts that ordinary citizens inhabited. Compared to Europe and Asia, these exactions were anything but onerous. Over and above them, there were the pervasive but *personal* and voluntary patron-client relations. The clients offered at a regular intervals gifts and services to their patrons in exchange for political protection and succour in times of need.

As is known, in tribal African societies the chief received prestations from his subjects as a sign of loyalty and, in turn, he was expected to help them when in need. This represented a public relation which was subject to communal control. In contrast, what happened between a patron and his client was individual and personal, and not subject to any external control. On the other hand, tribute, while public, was neither reciprocal nor subject to communal control. It was a prerogative of the political authority. Therefore, despite some apparent similarities, there is no real comparison between the forms of appropriation and use of value in tribal societies and in tributary and patron-client systems. Tributary and patron-client relations are not only hierarchical but are also *non-redistributary* in nature. The kings and their staff in the interlacustrine societies were under no obligation to channel back what they extracted from their subjects. Secondly, there was no communal control over the amount they could extract from their subjects. This created the possibility not only of a higher standard of living among the state officials but also for private accumulation. Whether or not this predisposition was fulfilled does not detract from the general principle. As has already been stated, patron-client relations, while not part of the state fiscal policy, created opportunities for private accumulation.

On the face of it, this method of extraction and accumulation of value complemented the more directly political method used by the state. It was convenient for the king to recruit powerful patrons into his bureaucracy, as they had influence locally or, at least, over their clients. Also, by making them his clients, the king stood to benefit from their accumulation. Nevertheless, influential chiefs with an independent power-base were a threat to the king. It is interesting to note that, universally, the monarchs in the interlacustrine resisted the development of private estates in the hands of their senior chiefs. They did this by making official estates non-heritable in principle i.e. official estates could not be passed on to the heirs of the incumbents without the approval of the king. In this context seizure of the assets of ambitious chiefs was not a capricious act. If local patrons were given an opportunity to reproduce themselves independently of the king, then the opportunities for the state to collect as much tribute from its citizens as it liked would have been seriously jeopardized. Increasingly, the patrons would have reserved the right to control the labour of those settled on their private estates, as happened under feudalism in Europe. The logical conclusion this leads us to is that there is a basic incompatibility between public appropriation of value in the form of tribute and private appropriation of value in the form of dues paid by clients to individual patrons. The latter would tend to undermine state power and reduce its capacity to organize extraction of tribute as general fiscal policy. On the other hand, it seems that in the interlacustrine kingdoms individuals entered into patron-client relations precisely to mitigate the despotic effects of the tributary state or to compensate for the loss of rights they enjoyed under the tribal system. It might be, Marx's error was not to refer to "despotism" in the Orient but to limit it only to that part of the world.

But did the patrons cushion off their clients from the worst effects of the tributary state? The answer is "yes". When individuals were in a desperate situation economically, socially and politically, they expected some help from their patrons and often got it in return for sustained exploitation under normal times. Nonetheless, all clients entered the relation with the expectation that their situation would improve such that one day they would gain their independence and become patrons in their own right. The fact of the matter is that no patron was interested in losing his clients or in helping them to become bigger than him. In other words, patrons saw to it that the net flow of goods and services was always in their favour. Therefore, the relationship between patrons and clients was not any less antagonistic than that between the tributary state and its subjects. In fact, it is evident that as long as the patrons themselves were dependent on the tributary state, they had to be serviceable to it. By maintaining the illusion that suppliant individuals were necessarily protected from its fangs, they inadvertently served the interests of the state. By personalizing the relations of exploitation, they effectively obscured potential class divisions. In practice the state did not always have to confront the general populace but exerted the necessary control through patrons who were vulnerable to its sanctions. Likewise, instead of imposing more and direct exactions on the producers, the king, patron of patrons, reserved the right to partake of the value patrons extracted from their personal clients. In the circumstance what was more visible were hierarchies of dyadic relations than would-be class relations.

Once again we are skating on slippery grounds. On the one hand, we admit that exploitation was general in the interlacustrine kingdoms and, on the other, we are disinclined to categorize, mechanically, all the exploiters as a class. This should be so. A deeper ethnographic and historical awareness should give us enough confidence not to be tyrannized by concepts. For example, "class-exploitation" presupposes the existence of classes, understood in terms of property and labour-relations. In the interlacustrine kingdoms as has been stated, property barely existed and had not been institutionalized in the majority of cases up to the end of the 19th century. For the same reason, labour-relations were wanting. At the domestic level the household-economy prevailed. At the public and non-domestic level political relations predominated i.e. value in the form of tribute and dues from clients was extracted solely by political and ideological means. Then, the logical choice is either to dispense with property - and labour-relations as a necessary, if sufficient, condition for defining "classes" or to conclude that the interlacustrine kingdoms were "pre-class" societies before contact with European capitalism.

Regarding the first alternative, it can be shown, historically, that, outside Europe, marked social differentiation had not necessarily been associated with ownership of property and direct exploitation of labour. Rather, in many parts of the world it had been contingent on *political control* over resources as well as people. Therefore, nothing much would be lost by relativising the Roman concept of property and the economistic or bourgeois concept of labour. The second alternative would only be a vindication of the dogma implicit in the first supposition about the necessity of property and labour-relations. As such, it would be a product of reification of concepts and not of historical analysis. We have already gone a long way to demonstrate that the interlacustrine kingdoms had passed the tribal stage which, we admitted, represented a classless society. We further observed that they were characterized by tributary and patron-client relations which did not readily fit into the conventional definition of class, unless all forms of exploitation were treated as identical. All patrons in the interlacustrine kingdoms can be presumed to have exploited their clients. The snag is that everybody, except the king and royal princes/princesses, was an actual or potential client. The rest remained a matter of degree: there were poor and richer clients in the same way as there were powerful and less powerful patrons.

It is evident that all patrons did not constitute a class. While small patrons were generally condemned to a lowly existence, the big patrons i.e. the "King's men" in the higher echelons of the bureaucracy, saw themselves as potential inheritors of official estates, at least, in the agricultural kingdoms. By the middle of the 19th century some had realized this dream, as witnessed by the rise of a landed aristocracy in kingdoms such as Buhaya and Bunyoro. Whereas the same thing could be said of the pastoral kingdoms, namely, that the "King's men" constituted a pastoral aristocracy or aspired to being pastoral aristocrats, fortunes in cattle wax and wane. Unlike the landowners, big cattle owners could not have hoped to reproduce themselves, without the patronage of the king. The herds of officials were increased more rapidly by raids and tribute than by breeding. The implicit insecurity of the pastoral aristocracy became more apparent under colonialism when these mechanisms for social reproduction were drastically curtailed. From this discussion it can be concluded that patron-client relations functioned relative to the tributary relation and that development of private property and individual opportunities for self-reproduction was essentially inimical to the system as a whole.

It can be stated, without prejudice, that up to the 19th century the interlacustrine kingdoms were organized around the principle of *tribute*. It was the manner in which tribute was extracted and used which defined the relationship between the rulers and the ruled. The ruled, whether patron or client, paid tribute to the state. It is significant that only royalty and territorial chiefs *bamasazza* or *bami* were exempted from such dues. They were unambiguously the *rulers*. Their mode of self-reproduction was strictly *political* i.e. control over people took precedence over direct control over productive resources. Any attempt by individual office-holders to reverse the situation would have been undoubtedly a subversion of the system and would have, inevitably led to the fragmentation of political authority or the state, as happened in feudal Europe. It is therefore not surprising that no monarch in the region was willing to countenance the prospect by surrendering ultimate control over all land in his territory. What is puzzling is the fact that Samir Amin in his theoretical schema considers European feudalism a variant of the tributary mode of production, even if "incomplete". At the level of property- and labour-relations or mode of appropriation of value, there is something definitely antithetical between feudalism and the tributary mode of appropriation of value. In fact, these were the grounds for rejecting the extension of the concept to sub-Saharan Africa especially. Secondly, the material from the interlacustrine strongly suggests that, historically, tributary relations were prior to any property-relations that might have emerged in the region during the 19th century. Finally, how do we explain the interposition of feudalism which was based on property-relations in land between tribal and tributary formations which were marked by communal or public control over land?

Logically and drastically, it would make more sense to suppose that the sequence was from tributary formations, and then to privatisation of land by the emerging political elite. This supposition is only true of the agricultural kingdoms in the interlacustrine. Furthermore, if it were assumed, as is traditional among Marxists, that "class-societies" are not only a later historical stage of development but are necessarily an improvement on "pre-class" societies, then European feudalism cannot be denied this privilege relative to tributary formations, as Samir Amin does in his definitive study[3]. Here, arguments get confused because of the difficulty of separating in reality between supra- and infra-structural elements. For instance, was European feudalism "incomplete" because of lack of centralized political authority or because of lack of development of material forces, compared to "complete" tributary formations? If we were to answer these questions in the context of the interlacustrine kingdoms, conflicting perspectives would emerge and, probably, force us to go back to fundamentals. For instance, apart from the problem of property and production relations, what is the nature of value and its historical implications in the societies under discussion? What is the relationship between particular forms of value and processes of development? Are certain values a necessary condition for development?

Up to the end of the 19th century the interlacustrine kingdoms were undoubtedly dominated by use value which was, universally, extracted by political means. Of the two political methods used, *tribute* was the dominant method. Not only was it consistent with public control of land resources but also signified the shift from reciprocal tribal economic relations to an extractive relationship, between rulers and anonymous subjects. In our view, patron-client relations, which were equally extractive, did not define the system. Rather, they were a result of the system and, potentially, its antithesis, if we take into consideration the fact that it was powerful patrons who were destined to erode the absolute power of the king and to interfere with the principle of tribute by seeking opportunities for individual or private appropriation of value. The political contradiction lies in the fact that the centralizing monarch in order to consolidate his power and to overcome the power of clan and lineage leaders needed, not powerful patrons, but rather effective clients in the form of an official bureaucracy (Buganda is the clearest example of this). But with the eclipse of the clan leaders, the ruled were left without any representation in the new set-up. Individuals began to look up to the King's clients for protection. The resulting patron-client relationship suited both parties, for the patron-chief gained greater political control through his clients and at the same time grew richer. Be it noted, however, that under the tributary system such prosperity was contingent on royal favour.

---

3   Samir Amin, *Class and Nation Historically and in the Current Crisis*, N.Y., 1980.

The last observation is meant to emphasize the overriding importance, economically and politically, of the tributary nature of the social relations in the societies under consideration. Extraction of value was politically controlled not for the benefit of the people as in tribal societies or of individuals as in the feudal societies, but for the benefit of the rulers whose embodiment was the state. But did the controllers of state-power by virtue of this constitute a *distinct-class*? In our view, they did not. The main reason is that the mechanisms for social reproduction were relatively undeveloped. First, the ability to raise state revenues was restricted by lack of mechanisms for converting tribute which consisted of only perishable goods into other utilities or values. Second, no precious stones or metals were in circulation. Cowry shells came only late in the 19th century and their impact was marginal. The reason for both failures was the general lack of markets, except in Bunyoro where there was limited trade before the arrival of the Arabs in the middle of the 19th century. Even when caravans reached Buganda and Bunyoro in the latter half of the 19th century, their rulers had no specialized goods to offer and were limited only to ivory and slaves. This was an outcome of a fairly low level of technological development. Because of lack of the art of writing, training remained informal and recruitment into official posts fairly unspecialized. Natural political skills are not sufficient in themselves to produce a self-perpetuating *esprit de corps*. Whether one agrees or not with our point of view, these various incapacities are a sufficient warning that we cannot infer class simply from extraction of value. What is diagnostic is the way value is realized and used i.e. the processes of reproduction and production. Until this point is reached, we can only think of classes in the process of becoming.

Our main conclusions can be summarized as follows:

a). In so far as the interlacustrine kingdoms had in the last three hundred years or so abandoned kinship as a basis for political organization and in so far as they had replaced reciprocal economic relations among kinsmen with extractive relations between rulers and the ruled, they had definitely ceased to be *tribes*. Accordingly, any tribal appellation that may attach to their various peoples must be treated as ideological "status-categories" which are subject to manipulation according to circumstances. We have the examples of the "Bairu", "Bahinda" and "Batutsi". If this manipulation is referred to as "tribalism", especially in the modern context, it must be acknowledged that it has nothing to do with the existence of tribes in the socio-historical sense.

b). In so far as there was no individual possession and disposition of property rights over land (dependent tenure), no seigniorial relationship between lord and vassal or serf for private exploitation of estates and in so far as no politically autonomous landlords had emerged to hold the balance of power within the social formation, the interlacustrine kingdoms cannot be described as *feudal*. Highly centralized political authority and possession of eminent dominion by the king over the whole territory is what they had in common.

c). In spite of a number of qualifications and relying on a limited number of basic principles, we are able to affirm that in their development the interlacustrine kingdoms had entered the tributary mode of production. This was achieved at different speeds but employing the same characteristic mechanisms. These include "tribute" as the organizational principle which defines both economic and political relations in society i.e. it is a mechanism for extracting economic value from the ruled as well as for maintaining relations of political domination. Second is absence of property-relations and accompanying labour-relations. This emphasizes the essentially extra-economic method of extracting value in tributary societies. Third is the dominance of use value, which is consistent with the second characteristic but does not preclude conversion of utilities from one form to another by whatever means. Other characterizations such as has been employed by Samir Amin, for example, state religion, dominance of the superstructure, tendency towards "stagnation" and propensity towards "expansionism" as a compensatory reflex against internal "losses" are either arbitrary or patently redundant. For instance, as is illustrated by the interlacustrine kingdoms, state ideology does not have to take the form of religion to exist at all. Similarly, "expansionist" policies are not any more peculiar to the tributary mode of production than subjectively defined "losses" are to other modes of production. Dominance of the "superstructure" is implicit in the idea that allocation of value in tributary formations is politically determined. "Political" is more precise than "superstructure" which might bring in a whole bag of cultural issues which might prove intractable. Similarly, "stagnation" is too relative a term to be definitive.

d). It would seem that the same grounds as are used for rejecting the concept of "feudalism" in reference to the interlacustrine kingdoms are sufficient for excluding feudalism from the historical category of tributary modes of production. The only feature it has in common with them is the dominance of use value. This is an important feature but it has to be weighed against another basic factor, namely, private property in land and direct exploitation of tied labour. We can ignore the last two features, only if we accept the radical suggestion made earlier that ownership of property is neither necessary nor inevitable for individual appropriation of value. In Africa we have the spectre of capitalist production on land that is held under customary tenure. Likewise, we have state capitalism which has served as an incubator for a budgeoning proto-bourgeoisie. The same could be said of individual appropriation under bureaucratic socialism in most of eastern Europe or of the so-called managerial class in Western Europe. *Effective control* over means of production is what seems to be essential. Ownership is just one variant of this and is not always effective. Think of the classical peasantry which owned some land but hardly had any effective control over the product of its labour.

e). For the time being, we note that not only did Samir Amin subsume feudalism under the tributary mode of production, without confronting this theoretical point, but also presumed it to be "incomplete" largely because of its fragmented political authority. This is tantamount to giving priority to superstructural features over infra-structural factors such as ownership of means of production and private appropriation of value - a procedure which is decidedly un-Marxist. If we credit Samir Amin's thesis that capitalism is a necessary stage of development, and that black Africa suffered stagnation mainly because of the persistence of communal land tenure which inhibited investment by individuals, then we must grant the fact that feudalism in this respect is nearest to capitalism than to tributary modes of production. Then, how could it be designated as "incomplete" and "backward"? Did the imposition of absolute monarchs in Europe complete it and thereby give it a longer lease of life? The best way of getting rid of these muddles would be to accept feudalism as a distinct mode of production which can be treated as not necessarily a precursor of capitalism, only if capitalism itself is not treated as a necessary condition for development to any other system, for example, socialism. In modern societies science and technology can be regarded as common property. What militates against this is, in fact, monopoly capitalism.

f). Regarding the question discussed above, it might be more appropriate rather to think of modes of production as in transition than incomplete. The answer to the question: when are modes of production complete? could be "when they are able to reproduce themselves indefinitely". But in so far as every mode of production is subject to decay due to internal contradictions, dynamically, there is no completion. However, conceptually there is, and there must be completeness, for incomplete concepts are perforce ambiguous. We included the interlacustrine kingdoms in the category of tributary modes of production because they met the specifications of a rigourously defined concept - tributary relations, political allocation of value, absence of property-relations and dominance of use value. While the tributary relationship was definitely antagonistic and involved exploitation, the rulers and the ruled did not immediately fall into distinct classes - one could be a chief today and a "peasant" tomorrow as in Buganda. We had to find reasons for this fluidity. They turned out to be relative undevelopment of the mechanism for reproduction and production. The conclusion from this is that classes in the interlacustrine kingdoms were still *inchoate* i.e. in the process of becoming. By the same token, none of the interlacustrine kingdoms can be accused of decadence or stagnation. The constant struggle by the bureaucracy to consolidate its control over originally solidary kinship groups and the attempts by senior chiefs to gain greater autonomy from the king are all a measure of the dynamism of these societies. It is important not to confuse such dynamism with the level of development of material and social forces. Compared to other tributary formations, the interlacustrine kingdoms up to the 19th century can be described as having been backward, especially the pastoral kingdoms amongst them. As has been pointed out, this reflected negatively on their capacity to resist the disruptive effect of colonialism or on that of the exploitative elite to take advantage of it, as happened elsewhere. This is a matter which we hope to pursue in the next chapter by examining a particular case, Buganda and the colonial encounter.

g). The level of development of material and social forces is supposed to determine the standard of living of members of society. But from historical experience we know that the benefits of development are rarely shared evenly. Distribution of goods and services is often skewed in favour of politically dominant groups, as in the interlacustrine kingdoms. Their capacity to take more than they actually produce is usually referred to as extraction of "economic surplus" or "surplus-value". In the text we have consciously avoided the use of either term and, instead, adopted the term, "economic value". Theoretically, "surplus-value" is inconceivable outside determinate production-relations which, we contended, did not obtain in the interlacustrine kingdoms. Once again, theoretically, all societies are capable of producing in aggregate more than they need for immediate purposes. This may be referred to as "economic surplus". But if disaggregated to meet the consumption needs of the privileged as well as the underprivileged, then there is no way in which we could objectively determine whether or not what was being extracted from the underprivileged was "surplus". To an ordinary pastoralist, what constitutes "surplus cattle"? When the tributary state obliges him to surrender some, all we know is that he has suffered extraction of *economic value*. From this premise we concluded that all producers in the interlacustrine kingdoms suffered extraction of economic value, without committing ourselves to the dubious and arbitrary notion of "economic surplus". This is important because under modern conditions many an African government has succeeded in pushing the peasantry below the subsistence level by insisting on extracting what is, ironically, referred to as "surplus". Genocidal exploitation can hardly be a measure of "economic surplus".

h). As regards our proposed concept of "social formation", it might be coincidental that the instance of political power and the instance of economics are unambiguously articulated through the tributary relation in the interlacustrine kingdoms, and not through two co-existent modes of production - pastoralism and "peasant" agriculture. But, logically and empirically, we seem to be on solid ground. In describing social formations as "communal", "tributary" or "capitalist", there is not the slightest suggestion that they might consist of more than one mode of production. What these terms indicate in normal discourse is modes of economic and political organization. Hence, our insistence that the concept of "social formation" denotes the articulation between the instance of power and of economics. This has made it possible for us in dealing with the interlacustrine kingdoms to put Buganda, characterized by a single mode of production (agriculture), in the same category as kingdoms which, according to popular notions, consisted of two modes of production - pastoralism and "peasant" agriculture. In our view, the tributary mode of organization overrode these apparent differences. Whether pastoralists or agriculturalists, the producers in the interlacustrine kingdoms were subject to the same principle. Secondly, whether realized through animal husbandry or cultivation, all production was geared towards subsistence. In so far as this is true, it is doubtful whether the cultivators were any more "peasant-like" than the pastoralists. It is our contention that, while pastoralists and cultivators represented different *modes of existence*, this did not necessarily signify different modes of production. Our case is vindicated by two factors, namely, interchangeability of the two modes of existence according to individual circumstances, and a combination of the two in the same hands in some of the kingdoms. Then, the inevitable conclusion is that neither pastoralism nor agriculture is a mode of production, but both are amenable to more than one mode of production, for example, the tributary and the lineage mode of production, as in the interlacustrian kingdoms.

i). Following on the above, it can further be concluded that the concept of "articulation of modes of production" is necessarily misleading because it treats co-existence of modes of production as characteristic of all social formations and, thus, minimizes the likely dialectical opposition between different modes of production, as will be shown later. Secondly, it could easily lead to the treatment of every mode of existence as a mode of production because it is synthetic and not analytical. It presents complex and abstract wholes such as modes of production as constituent elements of a social formation. By concentrating on the economic instance and the instance of power, which are both concrete, we were able to show that in the interlacustrian kingdoms pastoralism and agriculture co-existed not so much as distinct modes of production but as two modes of existence representing one mode of production, the tributary mode of production. As will be recalled, in this mode of production land is neither a subject nor a means of production but rather an instrument of production. However, our problem was whether to equate cattle directly with arable land.

Now, it seems reasonable to conclude that pastoralism is a way of appropriating not land itself, as some writers[4] have supposed, but only its manifestations, viz. pasture and water. In so far as the value so appropriated accrues solely to recognized corporate groups, namely, lineages, cattle can be regarded not as a communal but as a domestic possession in much the same way crops are among agriculturalists. In the event, contrary to Bonte's classical Marxian supposition, communal or pooled labour does not necessarily denote shared value. The apparent discrepancy between socialized labour, especially where the size of family herds is known to vary widely, and appropriation of its value would imply exploitation of the less endowed families. But this theoretically possibility is contradicted by the universal practice among African pastoralists of *loaning out cattle* to needy families within the community in order to sustain them or to start them off. This compensates the would-be exploited families and maintains a certain demographic balance between cattle and people or potential labour under conditions where individual chances for livelihood are nil. However, it does not eliminate inequality between different lineages - the primary units of affiliation in black Africa. Once the implicit inequality is transformed into

---

4   For example, Bonte in Kahn and Llobera, op. cit., pp. 23-32.

patron-client relationships as among the interlacustrian pastoralists, then it could be concluded that relations of exploitation have thus been instituted. Be it noted that, like tribute in these social formations, such social relationships are imposed by non-economic means. Otherwise, when this is achieved by economic means as in Buganda or Southern Ethiopia[5], it can no longer be referred to as "tribute" but more appropriately as "rent".

The significance of this observation lies in the fact that the mechanisms by which integration of different modes of existence or production are achieved signal qualitative transformations which may affect the transition from one mode of production to another. Therefore, the question is whether we can talk about dissolution of pre-capitalist modes of production and the introduction of the capitalist mode of production, without referring to the specific mechanisms involved. Whereas in the interlacustrian kingdoms the integration of the pastoralist and agriculturalist modes of existence was achieved by extra-economic means, leading to the establishment of the tributary mode of production in which use-value still predominated, under colonialism the same means do not seem to have ushered the capitalist mode of production in which exchange value is determinant. Is it the means that are at issue or is it the incompatibility between certain modes of existence and capitalism. Under colonialism agriculturalists readily adopted cash-crop production, whereas the pastoralists steadfastly refused to turn their cattle into means of production[6]. Does the objective need to capitalize both land and cattle at the same time render it harder for pastoralists than agriculturalists to make the necessary transition? Or is it a mistake to equate the two modes of existence under certain conditions? This is a problem which is worth pursuing, paying particular attention to processes of social reproduction of domestic groups or households under colonial capitalism, as Meillassoux did and will be done in a separate study.

j). The final methodological lesson that can be drawn from the study is that detailed ethnographic knowledge helps us to avoid mechanistic interpretations. Far from opening the way to relativism or particularism, it enables us to decode what might strike us at first sight as so many different things and, thus, puts us in a position where we can discover hidden unities. For instance, we discovered that tribal names were used, not to identify tribes, but to designate status-categories in non-tribal formations, for example, Bairu, "Batutsi". Furthermore, ethnographic

---

5   cf Crummey in Crummey, D., and Stewart, C.C., (eds.) *Modes of Production in Africa: the Precolonial Era*, 1981.
6   cf Rigby, P., *Persistent Pastoralists*, London, 1985.

detail showed that, contrary to the stereotype that pastoralists were the founders of the kingdoms in the interlacustrine region, neither the pastoralists nor the agriculturalists can take credit for this. Likewise, ethnographic detail forbids us to treat pastoralism and cultivation as things apart. The kingdoms were a result of a dynamic synthesis of social elements that were drawn from both traditions and the prevailing modes of existence within them served as politically-controlled alternatives. Consequently, political ascendency was not confined to the bearers of either tradition. These discoveries enable us to generate more objective codes and to put into proper perspective the historical and ethnographic intricacies of African societies. This is the best contribution African social scientists can hope to make towards a general theory of social development. Confirmation or refutation of existing theories must be informed by the historical and social reality of the various regions in the world, for it is from this that regional strategies for social action and development can be derived.

COLONIAL HERITAGE AND THE CRISIS OF AFRICAN SOCIAL FORMATIONS: THE CASE OF BUGANDA

As has been shown, the interlacustrine kingdoms had decidedly entered the tributary mode of production. Their dynamic drive towards the full realization of this mode varied from case to case, with the agricultural kingdoms having a certain edge on the pastoral kingdoms for reasons that have already been stated. As is known, towards the end of the 19th century all became victims of colonial imposition, irrespective of their level of development. Then, the intriguing question is whether or not their own internal structures became an important predisposing factor in subsequent developments. In radical literature there have been debates about processes of dissolution and preservation of African modes of production under colonial capitalism. This had been largely in reference to the so-called "subsistence sector" and its redistributive functions. However, it is apparent from our study that the term does not refer to any particular mode of production. Perhaps, it could be assumed that it referred to the tribal societies in which the lineage mode of production was the rule. This does not say anything about those African social formations which had passed the tribal stage. It might be of great theoretical interest to find out what was dissolved or preserved in social formations other than the tribal ones.

It is clear that in the tributary kingdoms of the interlacustrine area, clan or lineage elders had lost their dominance in the process of social reproduction to the centralizing monarchs. Therefore, processes of dissolution and preservation could not have referred but to the latter. In the event the mechanisms for achieving that goal could not have been the same as in segmentary societies. The absolute monarchs in the interlacustrine region were interested in the same thing as the colonialists i.e. extraction of economic value. While retention of their bureaucracies might have proved convenient, preservation of their power might have constituted a contradiction for colonial capitalism as well as future African petit-bourgeois governments. This would emphasize social incompatibilities rather than complementarities, as are seen by articulation theorists. In this connection Buganda is a suitable test case.

Of the interlacustrine kingdoms Buganda is by far the most well-studied. It received a great deal of attention because at the time of conquest it was among the most powerful in the region and by some accounts the most advanced kingdom in the interlacustrine. The latter referred mainly to its political organization and administrative structure. As will be recalled, by the middle of the 19th century the kings of Buganda had replaced the principle of hereditary chiefs with an appointed bureaucracy which was accountable only to the Kabaka. As a corollary to this, clan heads had been disposed of as local representatives and as land custodians in respect to their clansmen. Instead, the Kabaka had arrogated to himself the right to distribute land. Thus, tenure got associated with political appointments. In so far as the official estates were not heritable but remained crown property, we can talk of dependent tenure between the king and his officials. However, this was strictly a political relation. The chiefs did not stand in a labour-relation to the king. Rather, they were a bureaucracy which produced no direct value. The second type of dependent tenure was that between the chiefs and their clients. With the abolition of clan land, the ordinary people could gain access to land only through chiefs, i.e. over and above being clients, they became tenants of the chiefs as was the case in Bukoba and Bunyoro as well. Nevertheless, in Buganda especially *basenze*, as they were called, were not labouring tenants nor were they tied to their landlords, *bami*. This means that the tenant-relationship, though a dependent form of tenure, was conceptually *not feudal*, if exploitative.

The intention in this chapter is to determine as accurately as possible the impact of colonial capitalism on the tributary mode of production in Buganda and on the specific political and economic relations mentioned in the preceding paragraph. As is well-known, the closing years of the 19th century in Buganda were ones of absolute chaos. The primary cause was British colonial intervention. Predictably enough, in a centralized kingdom the first institution to suffer the slings of colonialism was the Kabakaship itself. Between 1877 and 1894, Buganda was forced to change kings four times. Pressure came from two directions. To ensure their overrule, the British wanted a pliant king. On their part, the different factions among the chiefs - Moslems, Catholics and Protestants - sought alliances with whomsoever they thought was the strongest patron. With the havoc that the maxim gun caused to the native armies, it was not too difficult to tell who was the strongest patron. The chiefs also had a vested interest in the diminution of the Kabaka's power. His "control" over all land in Buganda gave him an undue advantage. Each time an interregnum occurred either because the Kabaka had been deposed, revolted or was banished the senior chiefs conspired to divide the land among themselves. Indeed, when they got the regency during the reign of the child king, Daudi Chwa, they negotiated with the British Protectorate Government on their own behalf. The result was the famous or notorious 1900 Uganda Agreement, whereby a mere 4085 chiefs received an outright allocation of private estates amounting to 8430 square miles plus 573 square miles of official estates, 350 of which was later reserved for the Kabaka under the 1908 Possession of Land Law. Jointly, the estates constituted half of the total land area in Buganda and were measured in square miles, as the local term *mailo* indicates. To consolidate their power, the chiefs agreed with Sir Harry Johnston that the Kabaka's traditional gatherings with his favourite chiefs and courtiers be converted into a regular council, the *Lukiko*, attended by all senior chiefs and, at least, three notables from each county. This was aimed at reducing the ability of the Kabaka to deal at will with individual chiefs.

Although writers such as Jorgensen believe that all these events marked

> The start of the bourgeois revolution in Buganda which was to replace the absolute monarchy with a constitutional monarchy and transform land into a commodity[1],

such claims might prove too facile. For instance, the fight for land among the Baganda chiefs is proof of neither "their bourgeois concept of land tenure"[2] nor of the fact that

> Possession of land and usufructuary rights rather than possession of political office was the base of economic and political power in Buganda[3].

The Kiganda proverb, *omwmi tafuga taka, a fuga bantu* - "a chief does not rule land, he rules people", is perfectly consistent with the requirements of social reproduction in a tributary mode of production. There are no patrons without clients, and there can be no tribute without production. Hence, up to the 19th century no chief in the interlacustrine kingdoms could be rich or politically powerful, without a strong following. For either, each chief, as has been shown in the previous chapters, needed land both as a political domain and as an instrument of production. The Baganda chiefs, like their counterparts elsewhere in the interlacustrine, were actually aware of this. Consequently, when they were given a chance under the Uganda Agreement, they chose the most densely populated areas in Buganda. Yet,

---

1   Jorgensen, J.J., *Uganda: A Modern History*, N.Y., 1981,p. 47.
2   Op. cit. p. 50.
3   Op. cit. p. 47.

they had no immediate intention of converting their numerous tenants into labouring tenants. Instead, they looked upon them as *busulu* and *envujjo* (rent and tithe) paying tenants. In addition, they regarded them as their loyal followers, *basajja bange* (my men). Nothing was "bourgeois" either about their conception of land tenure or about the production relations they fostered.

However, even in pre-colonial days one thing that the Baganda chiefs had always fancied was tenure which was independent of the Kabaka. As had been noted in the case of Buhaya and Bunyoro, in the agricultural kingdoms there had already been a tendency towards heritable or private estates especially among territorial governors *bakungu*. In Buganda the most the Kabaka was prepared to do was to give out small private estates *obwesengeze* to individuals as rewards for special services. The drive towards private estates among the senior chiefs in the interlacustrine kingdoms was not created by the British. Through a combination of misconceptions on the part of the British and opportunism on the part of the Baganda Protestant chiefs in particular the process was precipitously pushed forward. Owing to its own internal dynamics, the system of official estates in the interlacustrine kingdoms was prone in the same direction. The question then is: what transformation would that have represented; or what kind of mode of production would it have given rise to? One of our conclusions in the last chapter was that feudalism, as a mode of production, is one step removed from the tributary mode of production. This was based on the fact that, unlike the latter, it was characterized by *private property* in land and *tied labour*. Furthermore, it was noted that, historically, it was marked by a fragmented mode of political organization. These might be used as indices to pin-point the kind of transformation that occurred in Buganda at the turn of the century, without assuming that it was necessarily feudalist or capitalist. For practical and theoretical reasons, it is still worthwhile maintaining the distinction made by Ernesto Laclau between participation in a "capitalist system" and participation in a "capitalist mode of production" in 1971.

In the literature dealing with the transition in Buganda since the beginning of the 20th century, it had been assumed that pre-colonial Buganda was "feudal" and that the landlords in post-colonial Buganda were "capitalist". This has been particularly true of the left, as is shown by the earlier quotations from Jorgensen's work. In a similar vein Mamdani, who is a declared Marxist, under a section entitled, "The Feudal Mode of Production" has this to say:

> In Uganda, the autonomy of this mode was lost with the destruction of the feudal state. But while the unity of the *class* was undermined, a

section of the feudal lords were *"sic"* reconstituted as landlords, subordinated to the colonial state. Whether legal or not, this process took place wherever the feudal mode prevailed in the south of Uganda. Where the precolonial ruling class had been the most powerful, in Buganda, the landed class retained a measure of autonomy from the colonial state until the second phase of colonial capitalism, the phase of its hegemony[4].

This statement is a comprehensive illustration of what we are alluding to. There had been further debates along the same lines between Mamdani and his adversaries, especially Nabudere[5]. Most of the discussion on the so-called capitalism in Uganda centred on commercial and finance capital rather than on production in the agrarian sector, which still constitutes the biggest sector of the national economy. This did not only deprive the various protagonists of an opportunity to test their own assumptions but also to bring out the specificity or anomalies of African modes of production under conditions of combined and uneven development.

On the face of it, British colonialism brought Buganda closer to the feudal mode of production than the indigenous system had done under the absolute monarchy. It did this by granting the incumbent chiefs allodial estates, which could be held independently of the Kabaka. The British did not only conceive of Buganda as a "feudal" society but were also interested in establishing a "landed aristocracy" as a counter-weight to the Kabaka who was the most likely focus of resistance to their imposition. The chiefs accepted the patronage of the British as long as it augmented their power by, for instance, granting them autonomous control over land and representative rights in a formally constituted *Lukiko*. Nonetheless, there is no evidence that they wanted a fragmented or decentralized state. Part of their power in dealing with the British and ultimately with Obote's nationalist government derived from the fact that Buganda was a centralized kingdom. Therefore, the Kabakaship was indispensable to them. This was to prove so even when they were challenged from within Buganda by the rising educated petit bourgeoisie in Mengo (the capital of the Federal Government of Buganda).

As far as labour-relations were concerned, the chiefs, as landowners, welcomed the British idea of a month's corvee labour *kasanvu* every year by the tenants on their private estates, instead of the traditional public

---

4   Mamdani, M., *Politics and Class Formation in Uganda*, N.Y., 1976, p. 139.
5   Nabudere, D.W., *Imperialism, the Politics of Class Formation and the National Question in Uganda*, Dar es Salaam, 1976; and *Imperialism and Revolution in Uganda*, London, 1980.

services which were not so prolonged. Neither they nor the British could sustain the system, as is shown by its abolition in 1921 due to continued protests from the tenants and to political reservations among some of the chiefs. Dues-paying tenants is what both patrons and clients were accustomed to in the tributary system. This had to be upheld with some adaptations which, far from eliminating the underlying contradictions, brought them out into the open. For the cultivation of cash-crops, the landlords needed regular labour. Dues-paying tenants did not meet this condition. One way of overcoming the problem was to introduce labour-tenants who generally came from Rwanda. They undertook to work for the landlords in exchange for a plot of land to meet their subsistence needs. They became tied labour not so much because they had no right of removal but mainly because they had no other means of access to land and, as immigrants, their bargaining power was weaker than that of the Baganda. The emerging labour-tenant relationships were more feudal than capitalist. However, we cannot be emphatic about this because payment in kind in a situation where commodity-relations were becoming general can also be regarded as a form of wages. Indeed, as time went on even the BanyaRwanda labour-tenants demanded some cash payment for their labour and received it, for there was competition for labour among the landlords. All this notwithstanding, it is arguable that the specifically feudalist elements in Buganda, namely, private estates divorced from public office, dependent tenure for the producers and semi-tied labour were a result of British colonial intervention. These lasted until, at least, 1928 when the *Busulu* and *Nvujjo* Law was passed by the colonial government. Nor should this be surprising. The same thing happened to the tributary formations in Latin America and India at the beginning of the colonial era. Owing to prevailing historical conditions, the changes in Buganda might have been more rapid and the mediations greater than in earlier examples. It is to these that we now turn.

Referring to the same problem Mamdani, in a rough and ready manner states:

> Whereas prior to 1928 the chiefs were landlords and their positions were hereditary, ... after 1928 they were without effective control over either their land or their position. Whereas before 1928 they were a class of landlords, after 1928 they were an intermediary state bureaucracy, a collaborating class that was dependent on, and identified with, the colonial state[6].

---

6   Op. cit., p. 127.

Not only is Mamdani's assertion factually inaccurate but also misses out on the dynamics of the situation. Since the middle of the 19th century, the *bakungu* chiefs i.e. the Kabaka's appointees had *never* held hereditary positions. Consequently, at no stage had they control over their positions; only the Kabaka did. Contrariwise, after 1928 they were as in control of *their land* as they had been since 1900. The reason is that all senior chiefs *(ssaza* and *gombolola* chiefs) were recruited exclusively from the landowning class. For political and ideological reasons, it was impossible in Buganda for one to be a notable or chief, *without land (etaka)*. It was superior tenure in land, irrespective of extent, which distinguished *bataka* (landowners) from *bantu buntu* or *bakopi* (ordinary people), or *bami* (landlords) from *basenze* (tenants).

Under these conditions, a non-landowner was a nonentity who could hardly hope to command the necessary respect and political influence. A great deal of the power the Baganda chiefs enjoyed derived from the political control they exercised over the local population which happened to be settled on their estates. It is true that after the 1900 Agreement the chiefs had become an intermediary colonial state bureaucracy and that they were a collaborating and dependent class. However this did not *ipso facto* eliminate their political power, as is shown by their dominance in the *Lukiko* throughout the colonial period and in the traditionalist *Kabaka Yekka* from the late 1950s until 1966 when Obote overthrew the Kabaka's government, and by their effective control in rural Buganda, despite continual attempts by the Buganda and the central government petit-bourgeois elite to oust them. Their dependence on and identification with the colonial government should not be exaggerated either. From 1952 to 1962 they fought a rear-guard battle against the colonial government which was preparing to make a deal with the emergent petit-bourgeoisie in Uganda at their expense. This led to a number of well-known constitutional and political crises in the country. Their suspicion of the colonial government and the local petit-bourgeoisie was not pure fantasy. It was based on their objective class interests. Contrary to Mamdani's supposition, their membership in the bureaucracy gave them the best opportunity for protecting their class interests. These interests they shared with other landowners who were not necessarily chiefs but all the same enjoyed considerable power in their domains.

It is, therefore, our submission that the landed class in Buganda, which was a creation of British colonialism, survived all attempts by the colonial state from 1928-1962 and by its petit-bourgeois successors from 1963 onwards to crush it. One of its main characteristics, which might be a problem of development, is that while it was interested in participating in the colonial capitalist system, it was basically *anticapitalist*. This is reminiscent of the *haciendados* and *latifundistas* in Latin America, who were a conservative but powerful force and were often dubbed as "feudalist" in the literature until the critical intervention by Rudolfo Stavehagen[7] and Gunder Frank[8]. It is, therefore, a question whether what has been referred to as a "landed aristocracy" in Buganda was a successor to the tributary mode of production or a precursor of a "capitalist" mode of production. In the meantime, we note that Sir Harry Johnston, the framer of the 1900 Agreement, had conceived of it as

> A practical attempt to establish on a sound basis a ruling oligarchy which, under British guidance, might do for Buganda what the *landed aristocracy* had done to give stability to the government of England[9].

Despite Johnston's illusions, it is a matter of record that the landed feudal aristocracy in England, far from being a source of political stability and growth, was in fact an impediment to both. The same might have happened in Buganda. Whereas in the early years after the introduction of cotton in Buganda in 1903 the landlord-chiefs showed enthusiasm and made their contribution by commanding their tenants to grow cotton in their newly acquired estates, by 1916 things had changed. According to Wrigley, cotton production had slipped out of the hands of the big landowners and had become an affair of scattered small producers who relied on their tenant plots for cultivation. By the mid 1920s the chiefs had successfully converted themselves into rentier-farmers. Not only did they collect rent from their tenants but also demanded tithes on any cash crops grown. Instead of the modest traditional tribute, their demands became ever so exorbitant and the chiefs were pushing for facilitating legislation in the *Lukiko*. Meanwhile, there was growing anxiety among the colonial administrators that any attempt to impose onerous demands on the tenants would discourage production. By 1925 the tide had turned against the landlords, who now were being described officially as "parasitic" or as a "forested plutocracy". In other words, they were not serving the interests of colonial capitalism well enough and they had to be replaced by another class. This turned out to be the peasant producers who were to form the basis of agricultural production in the Protectorate. The 1928 *Busulu* and *Envujjo* Law was passed specially

---

7   Stavenhagen, R., *Seven Fallacies about Latin-America* in J. Petras and M. Zeitlin (eds.), Latin-America: Reform or Revolution? N.Y., 1978.

8   Frank, G., *Capitalism and Underdevelopment in Latin-America*, N.Y., 1969.

9   As quoted by Mamdani, M., p. 41, italics added.

to entrench their rights and to curtail the demands of the landlords on them. The major effect of the law was to grant the tenants permanent and heritable rights over their tenancies. This was an important step, given the fact that up to 40 per cent of the land in southern Buganda was taken up by tenancies. Secondly, the labour-dues *busulu* to which the landlords were entitled were commuted into cash payments fixed at Shs.10, of which Shs. 1.50 was government levy on land. Finally, tithes or tribute *envujjo* on cash crops (cotton and coffee) was limited to Shs 4.00 per acre up to 3 acres. This was a peasants' charter which was designed to undermine Johnston's vaunted landed aristocracy.

This did not quite succeed, for in abandoning cotton the landlords gradually moved over to coffee production. Two factors favoured them. As a plantation crop, coffee needed relatively bigger plots of land than were usually available to tenants. Secondly, after the collapse of the forced labour system and the new confidence in the capacity of the natives to grow cash-crops in their own right, the colonial administration decided that it was not necessary to maintain a plantation system in Uganda in the hands of foreigners as in Kenya. The Buganda landowners were, thus, saved any unfair competition from European and Asian planters. Although tenants were not barred from coffee cultivation and contrary to Mamdani's belief that it was "grown predominantly on peasant farms", in fact it got strongly associated with big landowners. In interviews in the late 1960s the Baganda informants identified unambiguously cotton as a crop for small producers *balimi batono* or *balimi bulimi* and coffee as crop for big men or producers *basajja banene* or *basajja bagagga*. There are objective reasons for this division of labour. We have already referred to the question of scale. Secondly, up to 1938 when the price of coffee was lower than that of cotton, it took a much bigger volume of coffee to make the same value as cotton. Thirdly, cotton, which is an extremely labour-intensive crop, was under the prevailing technical conditions in Uganda better suited to small-scale production relying on family labour than on large-scale production relying on hired labour. In contrast, as Wrigley points out, robusta is a lazy man's crop. The climate was ideal for it in south-western Buganda and it needed very little attention. The landlords were saved the chore of supervising labour as well as the cost, except during the coffee-picking season. When the coffee prices went up dramatically from the late 1930s onwards, they reacted by engaging in extensive rather intensive cultivation. Most tenants could afford neither.

No doubt, the landlords contributed to cash-crop production in Buganda. But they did not become the leading economic class, as was envisaged by the colonial capitalist state. They perverted the system by continuously seeking non-capitalist methods for realizing value. Rent and tribute was the commonest of these under the system of *kibanja* tenancies. The second method was to use immigrant workers as labour-tenants, instead of using consistently wage-labour and endeavour to exploit directly more and more of their land. In cases where labour was regularly employed, it was partly looked upon as clients/followers or as servants/menial workers who produced very little added value. The third method which developed mainly after the Second World War was *kupangisa* (share-cropping). The land was normally rented out or leased for only one season usually to northern Ugandans who thereafter returned to their homes, without investing anything in the land. This prompted one land commissioner to remark that under the system the land was not "being farmed but being mined". The fourth method was to charge entry fees (*nkoko* = chicken) for new *bibanja* which, though illegal, appreciated in value as competition for land increased among tenant-farmers. From these arrangements, the landlords grew richer but brought about no capitalist revolution in agriculture. Technologically, they remained as backward as the small producers. Instead of reinvesting in agriculture, they were inclined to finance higher consumption and accumulation of *mailo* interests for their descendants. Consequently, in a survey carried in 1966 by the author and David Hougham, it was found that only 20 per cent of the land held by big landowners was under cultivation.

Despite this, there was progressive fragmentation of big estates, as more buyers who were willing to pay high prices for land came forward. Some of these arose from the ranks of sitting tenants who used the proceeds from their cash-crops for buying land. Otherwise, the routes to capital accumulation for purchase of land were many and diverse. In the survey just mentioned, petty trade especially in agricultural goods, haulage, village retail shops and petrol stations featured strongly. Employment in the bureaucracy far outweighed employment in commerce and industry as sources of capital accumulation. Most Baganda bureaucrats cherished the idea of retiring to a farm or retreating to one during holidays or weekends. It is, therefore, a serious sociological error to try and distinguish between "civil servants", "traders" and "kulaks", as Mamdani does in his study[10]. All these categories were perfectly interchangeable in Buganda. Traders invested in land, kulaks and traders invested in education for their children, and emerging bureaucrats invested in land as well as in education. This completed the cycle and signalled the rise of one and the same class, the

---

10   Op. cit., pp. 151-170.

African petit-bourgeoisie. It was this class which posed a challenge, politically and socially, to the landed oligarchy in Buganda. In agriculture they became known as "progressive farmers". They owned modest amounts of land, varying between 15 and 45 acres. For this precise reason, they preferred cultivation of all the land available to rent-paying tenants. Their ambitiousness drove them to greater personal effort and use of more intensive methods of production, for example, crop diversification, insecticides, manuring and nursery seedlings or seeds. Mechanical devices or animal traction and fertilizers were still a rarity even amongst them, perhaps for good reasons. The terrain in southern Buganda is ill-suited to mechanization and the soil, alluvial and deep up to 14 feet, is highly fertile.

Needless to say, these farmers were favoured by the colonial administration and received every kind of encouragement from it, for example, loans, technical inputs and advice. The Uganda Credit and Savings Bank for Traders and Farmers was established especially for their benefit in 1950. But the administration consciously excluded them from marketing and processing. This was a preserve for British and Asian companies through which unequal exchange was effected. The producers were aware of this. In 1941 they formed the Uganda African Farmers' Union, by which the Baganda kulaks or "progressive farmers" meant to advance their political and economic interests. They demanded the right to market their produce through their own marketing co-operatives. They also clamoured for the right to set up their own ginneries and coffee-curing factories. This was the extent of their economic fight against the colonial state. Politically, they were fighting on two fronts. They were fighting against the hegemony of the landlords in the County Councils and the *Lukiko*. At times this expressed itself as a division between Catholics and Protestants since the overwhelming majority of the *mailo* recipients in 1900 were Protestant chiefs. In reality it was petit-bourgeois interests against the interests of the traditional oligarchy. Later, these found expression in the two political parties in Buganda, the Democratic Party and the *Kabaka Yekka*, respectively. But certainly, the petit-bourgeoisie was on the ascendancy, regionally and nationally.

What emerges from the foregoing account is a highly distorted social formation. For instance, the landlords in Buganda were a recognizable class, thanks to the large individual estates they were granted by the British. However, what is striking about them is that they were neither bourgeois in economic and political outlook nor representative of the tributary mode of production. The separation by the ethocentric British between land and office had made sure of the latter. Meantime, the tenants, some of whom became what was known as "progressive farmers" were not only condemned at best to expanded petty commodity production but were also constrained by dependent tenure. They were neither a free peasantry nor holders of usufratuary rights under customary tenure. Thus, in their case as well the path to becoming an agricultural bourgeoisie was blocked. This is in spite of the fact that superficially, developments seemed to be in favour of private property. Although most of the farmers identified as "progressive farmers" in our 1966 survey were tenants, some had in the meantime purchased modest amounts of land or taken up more tenancies. Under the law private tenancies in Buganda are as good as ownership since they are held in perpetuity. Secondly, although some progressive farmers did with some family labour, wage labour played the major role. Finally, most of their production was aimed at making profit. This was so much so that they were referred to as capitalists *basajja bagagga* by the people in Buganda. This is a correct identification. But judged by their mode of investments and scale of operations, they must be classified as *small capitalists* or petit-bourgeoisie.

Economically, they are a weak class. Not only are they a tiny minority among the rural producers (about 5 per cent) but also do not represent any capital in particular, as is evidenced by their moving back and forth between agriculture, trade and bureaucracy. As far as processes of accumulation are concerned, they are squeezed by imperialism through unequal exchange and finance capital. As far as landownership is concerned, they are kept on a leash by the landlords who see them as upstarts. In fact, there had been a continuous struggle between them and the landlords for political control. Their representatives in the Buganda government were quite open about it:

> The only way to defeat the chiefs is to keep re-posting them so that they do not develop roots and to give them early retirement.

This was wishful thinking as long as the chiefs and their fellow-landlords owned most of the land in Buganda. As one chief put it,

> We are rooted on the land and we cannot allow dispatching clerks and porters to rule us.

It is, therefore, apparent that the landlords and the commercial farmers represent antagonistic class interests. What is even more striking is the fact that, though both have participated in a capitalist system for about half a century, neither can be described as representative of the *capitalist mode of production*. This is an important reminder to those who so easily talk about a "bourgeois revolution" having occurred in Buganda or Uganda in general. What might have occurred so far is a petit-bourgeois "revolution", if we grant that the leading social class so far has been the petit-bourgeoisie. What of the proletariat and the peasantry, it may be asked.

After 1928 peasants in Buganda were meant to be the foundation of the agricultural economy. Indeed, they participated vigorously in cash-crop production, while not abandoning subsistence-crop production. Their share in the total volume of agricultural production was highest due to their sheer numbers and hard work. However, their tenant plots were generally small, averaging about 3 acres. Their technological inputs were almost zero and their capacity to raise loans for agricultural improvements was limited by the fact that they had no title deeds to the land they cultivated which they could offer as collaterals to the banks. The petit-bourgeois dominated cooperatives were inclined to exploit them mercilessly whenever they turned to them for help. They were heavily taxed by the colonial and the petit-bourgeois state after independence through marketing boards, receiving virtually nothing in exchange. As the years went by, they became despondent and agriculture began to show signs of stagnation. It was then that the idea of "progressive farmers" was introduced in the 1950s. They were supposed to replace the peasantry which had come to a full-stop. Ironical as it may sound, exploitation and neglect by both the colonial state and the petit-bourgeois governments after independence and the rapaciousness of the commercial farmers, all served to reinforce the faith of the peasantry in Buganda in their landlords. The landlords exploited them as much as anybody else but gave them a certain amount of security or protection in the context of the traditional patron-client relations. When individuals were in difficulties, they turned to their landlords for help. They often got it, but not without increasing social and financial indebtedness.

It was interesting to listen to tenants giving their reasons for not taking up Obote's offer of *rent-free* tenancies or leases on the sequestrated official mailo land after the 1966 coup. What it boiled down to was that they could not rely on the central government and could not afford to antagonize the landlords in Buganda by accepting favours from their (class) enemy. This is not how they reacted when the colonial government entrenched their rights by law in 1928. It saved them from abuse by private landlords who were not as dependent on them, politically, as the chiefs used to be under the *ancien regime*. Secondly, it was considered fair as the chiefs had under the 1900 Agreement been given land that did not belong to them. All the same, their being tied to the landlords breeds conservatism amongst them. It is not uncommon for peasants to be conservative ideologically. What is unique about Buganda is that it is probably the only region in black Africa which has no *free peasantry*. This highlights the negative implications of the continued existence of a non-bourgeois landowning class in Buganda. The landlords in Buganda have neither been transformed nor expropriated. Out of weakness, the petit-bourgeoisie has been playing cat and mouse with them since independence.

In addition to rent-tenants, there were in Buganda labour-tenants and casual workers who appeared during the peak season. Most of these, as was mentioned earlier, were immigrant workers. As would be expected, they were less tied to the Baganda landlords. In the 1960s they showed a preference for the commercial farmers. The latter had a reputation for working hard their labour but for higher and regular wages. This strict contractual relationship gave the workers the freedom to move from one farmer to another, according to their convenience. They were hardly involved with the Baganda, including the tenants and the few Baganda agricultural workers. The Baganda peasants are noted for their resistance against being proletarianized. Their ambition was always to get hold of a tenant plot in which they could work on their own behalf. Failing this they look for jobs outside agriculture. So, if they counted as a proletariat, they counted more as such in the urban areas than in the countryside. This left the immigrant workers in the rural Buganda with no local leadership and, as outsiders, were liable to community blackmail. Consequently, even though privately they supported the views of some of the national parties or of the government, they would not expose themselves. This means that, like the Baganda tenants, they were politically handicapped. Hence, the field was left open to the petit-bourgeoisie and the landed aristocracy. This is in contrast to the urban areas where the contending classes were the petit-bourgeoisie and the workers who were highly unionized.

In the context of our study of the tributary mode of production, its predispositions and transformation under colonial capitalism, what we learnt from the case of Buganda can be summarized as follows:

a). The tributary class which was already straining at the leash to take possession of the official estates will do so at the first opportunity. In Buganda and elsewhere in the interlacustrine that was the major bargaining point of the chiefs. This was made the more the easier by the fact that the power of the traditional monarchs had to be undermined as a necessary condition for colonial imposition. Having got the land, the chiefs in Buganda and elsewhere, as a collaborating class, were used in the subjugation and domination of the rest of the population. But as they were more interested in maintaining their traditional privileges (which were based on use-value and personal services) than in fostering colonial capitalism, they fell foul of the colonial state and they had to be jettisoned.

b). This proved rather difficult because individual ownership of land and political control over tenants gave them a tremendous advantage. They used this with great skill to resist further pressure from the colonial government and to frustrate the modernizing petit-bourgeois elite. This is a case where contrary to Samir Amin's hypothesis, individual land tenure did not lead to development or technological advancement. Instead, it led to monopolization of land resources by an unproductive class of landlords. It is probable that the class in charge is more critical than mere private ownership of land, as was suggested in the main text.

c). With the breaking up of the tributary state and the ensuing free for all, the peasants should have been able to hang onto some of the land they held under the lineage system or in the domains of nonhereditary chiefs and were using for subsistence production and for paying tribute. As the land was plentiful in most of the interlacustrine kingdoms, they should have also been able even to buy some land at relatively low prices. In this way an independent peasantry would have emerged, as happened except in Buganda. In Buganda the division of the whole country between the incumbent chiefs and the British Crown deprived the peasants *ab initio* of any independent rights in land. In this way they got beholden to the landlords and became unavailable to the other classes for political mobilization.

d). For production for the colonial state the alternative to the discredited tributary chiefs was the peasants. Everywhere the peasants were obliged to meet the demands of the colonial state. However, for the purposes of administration, services and other technical functions, it needed literate cadres. This gave rise to the petit-bourgeoisie, a new breed, which was derived from all sections of society. Its interests coincided with those of the colonial state and were opposed to those of the landlords and the peasants. The colonial government encouraged this class to play an intermediary role in agriculture, commerce and in the bureaucracy. In Buganda it was constrained not only by imperialism but also by the landowning class. Elsewhere in the interlacustrine it had fairly good opportunities for acquiring land but it never developed into a national agricultural bourgeoisie. The same is true of commerce. But everywhere it became a leading class, politically. Whatever the weaknesses of this class, they are not attributable to the pre-existing social formation as it did not exist then. The ultimate explanation must be that the petit bourgeoisie in the ex-colonial countries is a child of imperialism and is encumbered with all the contradictions this implies.

It is Samir Amin's "third force", but extraverted and unbourgeois in its economic behaviour.

e). What we witnessed in Buganda, the most advanced kingdom in the interlacustrine, is a social formation which has lost all its former coherence as a result of colonial intervention. Under colonial tutelage class struggles between landlords and tenants, between landlords and the rural petit-bourgeoisie and between the landlords and the national petit-bourgeoisie could not be resolved. After nearly a hundred years of participation in a capitalist system, no agricultural revolution has occurred in Buganda (there might have been even regression towards monoculturalism compared to the situation in the 19th century).

In the circumstances there is no objective reason why a country which aspires to a socialist transformation has to go through a capitalist stage which has proved unrealizable under imperialism. Or is it a question of perpetuating Marx's unjustified supposition that the introduction of capitalism in countries such as India would deliver them from "centuries-long stagnation and propel them into the modern age"? Underdeveloped countries have been part of the capitalist system for a good 100 to 200 years, without being able to overcome their underprivileged status and stunted growth. It is obvious that their problem at this historical juncture is how to break out of a system which works inexorably to their disadvantage. However, the issue cannot be easily resolved because within each country, as we saw in the case of Buganda, various classes view the struggle differently. In other words, there is a disjuncture between the historically determined contradiction at the global level and subjective class interests at the national level. Therefore, it is undoubtedly the resolution of the national question which will determine the direction in which each country moves.

None of these classes represents a particular mode of production. The tributary mode of production in which the political instance was dominant and in which economic production was determined by use value had been dissolved in two important ways. First, the tributary rulers had been usurped by the colonial power and the tributary relationship between them and the producers abolished. Second, the separation between office and land gave rise to a rentier class of landlords who relied partly on hired labour and labour-tenants for production for the market.

In this way they realized *surplus value* for individual-appropriation. Therefore, it can be said that the tributary mode of production in Buganda did not survive colonialism. What survived is the patron-client relationship in the rural sector. This was made easier by the absence of an independent peasantry since all the land had been converted into private estates held not so much by chiefs any more but by individual landlords. Contrary to expectation, the landlords did not use their estates to increase productivity in agriculture by intensifying technological factors. Instead, they became largely rentier farmers, getting enough in volume from what was otherwise a fairly low level of productivity. In other words, they did not make the transition to the capitalist mode of production. Worst still, they used their monopoly over land and their political power to frustrate those who wanted to engage in serious capitalist production so as to gain economic and political power. This is what we referred to as a drifting rural petit-bourgeoisie. What is worth noting here is that, contrary to Samir Amin's postulate, private ownership of land and disappearance of "communal" ownership in Buganda did not lead to the rise of capitalism and the introduction of advanced production techniques.

If, as we maintain, the landowners in Buganda were neither representatives of the tributary mode of production nor agents of the capitalist mode of production, then what was the fate of the other rural classes under colonialism? As was mentioned, the tenants farmers operated within the confines of the expanded petty commodity mode of production. Even this they did not do with any persistence. They fluctuated between petty commodity production and circulation in the form of petty trade. At times because of unfavourable external market prices or government pricing policy implemented through the extractive marketing boards, they were forced to seek employment in the urban areas or in the bureaucracy. So, they were neither a settled free peasantry, an emerging rural merchant class, nor a rural or urban proletariat. Like the landlords, they were products of colonial capitalism and represented no particular historical class. This makes it impossible to characterize the mode of production in Buganda in conventional terms. It is neither tributary nor capitalist. Then, what do these malformed classes represent in their combination?

To those who advocate the theory of "articulation of modes of production", the answer might seem obvious. However, if the basic supposition is that the articulation takes place between *modes of production*, then with the *dissolution* of the tributary mode of production under colonialism and the failure to develop *capitalism* in its place such could not have occurred in Buganda. What actually took place was the introduction of capitalist exchange relations and individual property. But both did not change fundamentally the labour process. Patron-client relations persisted, combined with labour-tenancies, seasonal hired labour and family labour. For a mode of production to be recognized as such, it must be able to reproduce itself consistently over a long period of time. This hinges on how labour value is generated and used. Despite all these gaps and inconsistencies, it still has to be conceded that as a result of colonial imposition Buganda became part of the *capitalist system*, without itself realizing the capitalist mode of production. This is a measure of its underdevelopment. This has been referred to as "underdeveloped capitalism" or "colonial capitalism" - all indicating its regressive character. If so, can it be seen as a dialectical successor of the outmoded tributary mode of production and a necessary stage for further development? If it is genuine capitalist development that theorists such as Samir Amin have in mind, how can this be realized under imperialism which is itself an antithesis capitalism? Logically and historically, how can we distinguish between the capitalist mode of production and its external manifestations which have provoked a deep and continuing economic and political crisis in ex-colonial Africa and elsewhere?

In examining this question our starting point cannot be modes of production, which are not yet identifiable, but rather the prevailing social formation. As has been argued, this is best understood as the articulation between the economic instance and the instance of power, including ideological reproduction. In Buganda the landlords controlled the most important economic asset, land. Through this, they held most of the rural population to ransom but justified it in terms of patron-client relations which under colonialism took the form of landlord/rent or labour-tenant. However, politically, they were being challenged very strongly by the new educated petit-bourgeois elite who were, otherwise, weaker economically i.e. they had no economic assets but lived largely on revenue. This is precisely what their political struggle was about: to capture state power so that they could have guaranteed access to national revenues. Under the impact of the nationalist struggle for independence, they came on top and used the state as an instrument for individual accumulation. The loot was spent on conspicuous consumption, petty trade, speculation in housing, and farms for "retirement". They did not expropriate the unproductive landed oligarchy for fear of a whole-scale rural rebellion, including the peasant clients who had less faith in them than in their tested landlords. Afterall, it was the government which was siphoning off economic value from the peasants through its resented marketing boards. Under these conditions no real capitalist class emerged and the disarticulation between the economic and political instance continued, giving rise to social instability. Eventually, this gave way to military coups and foreign interference.

While the struggle between a parasitic modern bureaucracy and conservative rural notables lasts, it is the direct producers who suffer most. But as their political support and continued production is essential to any class which seeks lasting hegemony, it is apparent that they will be the ultimate arbiters in any future struggles. Nonetheless, even this is not altogether guaranteed, as they are often overruled by imperialist forces on behalf of classes which seek to maintain the status quo, for example, in Angola, Mozambique, and the rest of southern Africa. Thus, the national struggle against colonial capitalism is inextricably bound with the struggle against imperialist domination in general. Consequently, it cannot be claimed in all seriousness that these struggles predicate the necessity of capitalism but rather its negations or antithesis. What precise form the latter will assume is an open question. One thing certain is that any kind of imposition, socialist or capitalist, will not work, as contemporary history shows. Autonomous development, involving the majority of the people, is what seems to hold the best prospects for a genuine social revolution. But is our understanding of the social and cultural connotations of the various regional responses to these historical developments deep enough for us to be effective interlocutors?

BIBLIOGRAPHY

Althusser, L. and Balibar, E., *Reading Capital*, NLB, London, 1970.

Amin, Samir, *Underdevelopment and Dependence in Black Africa: Historical Origins*, JMAS, 10, 4, 1972.

Amin, Samir, *Class and Nation Historically and in the Current Crisis*, Monthly Review Press, New York, 1980.

Arrighi, G., *The Relationship between the Colonial and the Class Structures: A Critique of Gunder Frank's Theory of the Development of Underdevelopment*, IDEP, Dakar, 1971.

Ashe, Robert W., *Chronicles of Uganda*, London/New York, 1894.

Banaji, J., "Frank in Retreat?" in P. Limqueco and B. McFarlane (eds), *Neo-Marxist Theories of Development*, St. Martin's Press, New York, 1983.

Beattie, J., "The Nyoro" in A.I. Richards (ed.), *East African Chiefs*, Faber & Faber, London, 1959.

Beattie, J., "The Kibanja System of Land Tenure in Bunyoro", *Journal of African Administration*, 6, 1954.

Beattie, J., *Bunyoro, an African Kingdom*, New York, 1960.

Beattie, J., *The Nyoro State*, Oxford University Press, Oxford, 1971.

Bernstein, H., et al, *Development Theory: Three Critical Essays*.

Bernstein, H., et al, *Underdevelopment and Development*, Penguin Books Ltd., Harmondsworth, 1973.

Bernstein, H., et al, and Nicholas, H., "Pessimism of the Intellect, Pessimism of the Will", *Development & Change*, 14, 4, 1983.

Bikunya Peter, *Ky'abakama ba Bunyoro* (History of Bunyoro), London and Kampala, 1927.

Bonte, P., *Marxist Theory and Anthropological Analysis* in Kahn and Llobera, 1981.

Brenner, R., "The Origins of Capitalist Development: a Critique of Neo-Smithian Marxism", *New Left Review* No. 14, July-August, 1977.

Brett, E.A., *Colonialism and Underdevelopment in East Africa*, NOK Publishers, New York, 1973.

Browett, J., "Into the Cul-de-Sac of the Dependency Paradigm with A.G. Frank", *Australia and New Zealand Journal of Sociology*, 1982.

Browett, J., "Out of the Dependency Perspectives", *Journal of Contemporary Asia*, 12, 2, 1981.

Buliggwanga, E.M., *Ekitabo Kye Kika Kye Mamba* (History of the Lungfish Clan), Kampala, 1916.

Bundy, E., "Uganda's New Constitution", *East Africa Journal*, July 1966.

Burton, R., *The Lake Regions of Central Africa: a Picture of Exploration*, London, 1860; repr. New York, Horizon Press, 1961, 2 vols.

Cardoso, F.H., *Current Theses on Latin American Development and Dependency: a Critique*, Dag Hammarskjold Foundation, Uppsala, 1977.

Carter, W. Morris., "Report on land tenure in the kingdom of Buganda", *Africa*, 869, 1906.

Chilcote, R.H., "A Critical Synthesis of Dependency Literature", *Latin American Perspectives*, 1, 1, Spring, 1974.

Claessen, H. And Skalnik, P. (eds.), *The Early State*, Mouton, The Hague, 1978.

Coleman, J.S. & Rosberg, C.G. (eds.), *Political Parties and Nationalism in Tropical Africa*, Univ. of California Press, Los Angeles, 1966.

Colvile, Sir Henry E., *The Land of the Nile Springs*, London and New York, 1895.

Cook, Sir Albert, *Uganda Memoirs*, 1897-1940, Kampala, 1945.

Cooper, J.D.O., *The Zulu Aftermath: A Nineteenth Century Revolution in Bantu Africa*, London, 1966.

Coquery-Vidrovitch, C., "The Political Economy of the African Peasantry and Modes of Production" in Gutkind and Wallerstein (eds.) *The Political Economy of Contemporary Africa*, Sage Publications, London, 1978, (first published in French in 1969).

Coquery-Vidrovitch, C., "Research on an African Mode of Production" in D. Seddon (ed.) *Relations of Production*, Frank Cass, London, 1978.

Cox, A.H., "The Growth and Expansion of Buganda", *Uganda Journal* 14/2 (1950), 153-9.

Crazzolara, the Rev. J.P., *The Lwo*, 3 vols. Vienna, 1950-54.

Crummey, D. and Stewart, C.C., (eds.), *Modes of Production in Africa: The Precolonial Era*, Sage Publications, London, 1981.

Curtin Philip., *Images of Africa: British Ideas and Action, 1785-1870*, University of Wisconsin Press, 1964.

Ddiba, J.L., *Eddini Mu Uganda*, Masaka, 1955.

Doornbos, M.R., *Not All the King's Men*, Mouton, The Hague, 1978.

Dunbar, R.A., *A History of Bunyoro-Kitara*, Oxford University Press, Nairobi, 1965.

Dunbar, R.A., *Omukama (King) Kabarega*, Kampala, East African Literature Bureau, 1965.

Dupre, G. and Rey, P.P., "Reflections on the Pertinence of a Theory of the History of Exchange", *Economy and Society*, 2, 2, 1973.

Dupre, G. and Rey, P.P., in Seddon (ed.), *Lineage Mode of Production*, 1973

Elkan, W., *An African Labor Force*, East African Studies, No. 7, 1956.

Elkan, W., *Migrants and Proletarians*, OUP, London, 1961.

Fallers, L.A., *Bantu Bureaucracy*, W. Heffer & Son, Cambridge, 1956.

Fallers, L.A., "Despotism, Status and Social Mobility in an African Kingdom", *Comparative Studies in Society and History* 2/1 (1959).

Fallers, L.A., *The Eastern Lacustrine Bantu*, London, 1960.

Fallers, L.A., "Are African Cultivators to be called 'Peasant'?", *Current Anthropology*, 2, 2, April, 1961.

Fallers, L.A., "Equality, Modernity and Democracy in the New States", in *Old Societies and New States* (Ed. C. Geertz). Glencoe, London, 1963.

Fallers, L.A., (ed.) *The King's Men*, London, 1964.

Fernandez, R.A. & Ocampo, J.F., "The Latin American revolution: A Theory of Imperialist, Not Dependence", *Latin American Perspectives*, 1, 1, 1974.

Fisher, A.B., *Twilight Tales of the Black Baganda*, London, 1912.

Fletcher, T.B., "Mwanga: the Man and His Times", *Uganda Journal* 4/1 (1936), 162-67.

Ford, J. and Hall, R.Z., "The History of Karagwe", *Tanganyika Notes and Records*, 24 (1947).

Foster-Carter, A. "Neo-Marxist approaches to development and underdevelopment", *Journal of Contemporary Asia*, 3, 1, 1973.

Forts, M. and Evans-Pritchard, E.E., (eds.), *African Political Systems*, Oxford, 1940.

Frank, A.G., *Capitalism and Underdevelopment in Latin-America*, Monthly Review, N.Y., 1969.

Frank, A.G., *Dependence and Underdevelopment*, Doubleday, NY, 1972.

Frank, A.G., *Crisis in the World Economy*, Holmes and Meier Publishers, New York, 1980.

Frank, A.G., *Critique and Anti-critique: Essays on Dependence and Reformism*, Praeger, N.Y., 1984.

Fortt, J.M., "The Distribution of Immigrant and Ganda Population within Buganda", in *Economic Development and Tribal Change* (ed.) A.I. Richards, W. Heffer & Son Cambridge, 1954.

Gale, H.P., 'Mutesa: Was He a God?' *Uganda Journal*, 20/1 (1956).

Gale, H.P., *Uganda and the Mill Hill Fathers*, London, 1959.

Gee, T.W., 'A Century of Mohameddan Influence in Buganda, 1852-1951', *Uganda Journal*, 22/2 (1958).

Gertzel Cherry, "Political Parties in Uganda", *Africa Report*, Oct., 1964.

Gingyera-Pinycwa, A.G.G., *Monarchism and Anachronism*, EAJ, Nov., 1967.

Gingyera-Pinycwa, A.G.G., *Prospects for One-Party System in Uganda*, FAJ, Oct. 1968.

Godelier, M., *Rationality and Irrationality in Economics*, NLB 1972.

Godelier, M., "On the Definition of a Social Formation", *Critique of Anthropology*, 1, 1974.

Godelier, M., *Marxist Perspectives in Anthropology*, Cambridge University Press, Cambridge, 1977, (first published in French in 1973).

Gomotoka, J.M.T., (Description of Kiganda Crowns in) Munno (1914).

Gomotoka, J.M.T., *Magezi Ntakke* (Short History of Buganda), White Fathers, Bukalasa, Uganda, 1930.

Goody, J., *Technology, Tradition and the State in Africa*, Oxford University Press, London, 1971.

Gorju, J., *Entre le Victoria, l'Albert et l'Edouard*, Rennes, 1920.

Grant, R.J., *A Walk Across Africa, or Domestic Scenes from My Nile Journal*, London and Edinburgh, 1814.

Gray, Sir John, 'The Basoga', *Uganda Journal* 3/4, 1936.

Gray, Sir John, 'The Early History of Buganda', *Uganda Journal*, 2/4 (1935).

Gray, Sir John, 'Mutesa of Buganda', *Uganda Journal* 1/1 (1934).

Gray, Sir John, 'Sir John Kirk and Mutesa', *Uganda Journal* 15/1 (1951).

Gray, Sir John, 'The Solar Eclipse in Ankole in 1492', *Uganda Journal* 23/2 (1963).

Gray, Sir John, 'The Year of the Three Kings of Buganda', *Uganda Journal* 13/2 (1949).

Gulalp, H., "Frank and Wallerstein Revisited: A Contribution to Brenner's Critique" in Limqueco, P. and Mc-Farlane, B., (eds.), *Neo-Marxist Theories of Development*, St. Martin's Press, New York, 1983.

Gutkind, P.C., & Wallerstein, I. (eds.), *The Political Economy of Contemporary Africa*, Sage Publications, London, 1976.

Gutkind, P.C., *The Royal Capital of Buganda: A Study of Internal Conflict and External Change*, The Hague, 1963.

Hammond-Tooke, W.D., *The Bantu-Speaking Peoples of Southern Africa*, Routledge & Kegan Paul, London, 1974.

Hopkins, A.G., "On Importing Andre Gunder Frank into Africa", *African Economic History Review*, 2, 1, Spring, 1975.

Huntingford, "The Peopling of the Interior of East Africa by its Modern Inhabitants", in R. Oliver and Q. Mathew (eds.), *History of East Africa*, Oxford Univ. Press, Oxford, 1963.

Ingham, K., *The Making of Modern Uganda*, London, 1958.

Ingham, K., 'Some Aspects of the History of Western Uganda', *Uganda Journal*, 21/1 (1957).

Johnston, Sir Harry H., *The Uganda Protectorate*, London, 1902, 2 vols.

Johnston, Sir Harry H., "A Survey of the Ethnography of Africa and the Former Racial and Tribal Migrations in that Continent", *J. Roy Anthrop. Inst.*, 43 (1913).

Jorgensen, J.J., *Uganda: A Modern History*, St. Martin's Press, N.Y., 1981.

Joy, L., "Mechanical Cultivation in Uganda", Proc. of Symposium of Mechanization, Makerere University College, Kampala, 1957.

Joy, L., "One Economist's View of the Relationship between Economics and Anthropology", in *Themes in Economic Anthropology* (ed. R. Firth). Tavistock Publications, London, 1967.

Kabuga, C.E.S., 'The Genealogy of Kabaka Kintu and the Early Bakabaka of Buganda', *Uganda Journal* 27/2 (1963).

Kagame, Abbe, A. *Les Milices du Rwanda Precoloniale*, Brussels, 1963.

Kaggwa, Sir Apolo, *Ekitabo Kya Basekabaka be Buganda*, 1, 1901, 1927, 1953. (See *Uganda Notes*, Jan, 1902: also review of 1912 edn. by J. Roscoe in *Man*, 27, 1914.

Kaggwa, Sir Apolo, *Ekitabo Kye Mpisa za Baganda*, London, 1918, reprinted 1952.

Kaggwa, Sir Apolo, *Ekitabo Kye Bika Kya Raganda*, Kampala, 1949.

Kaggwa, Sir Apolo, *Empisa Za Baganda* (The Manners and Customs of the Raganda), London, 1905: reprinted 1918, 1952.

Kaggwa, Sir Apolo, *Ebika Kya Baganda* (1912), reprinted Kampala, 1949.

Kaggwa, Sir Apolo, *Ekitabo Kye Kika Kyensenene* (The History of the Grasshopper Clan), n.d. (1900) privately printed on the author's press.

Kakoma, G. et al., *Ekitabo Eky A'bakyanjove Abe Mamba Mussiga Iya Nankere e Bukerere*, Kampala, East African Institute of Social Research n. d.

Karugire, S., "Relations between Bairu and Bahima in 19th Century Nkore", *Tarikh* 3, 1970.

Karugire, S., *A Political History of Uganda*, Heinemann, Nairobi, 1980.

Karugire, S., *A History of the Kingdom of Nkore in Western Uganda to 1896,* Clarendon Press, Oxford, 1971.

Kasfir, N., 'The Decline of Cultural Sub-nationalism in Uganda". Makerere University College, Kampala, mimeo, n.d.

Kasfir, N., *The Shrinking Political Arena*, California Univ. Press, Los Angeles, 1976.

Kasirye, J., *Obulamu bwa Stanslaus Mugwanya* (A Biography of Mugwanya), London, 1962.

Kasitye, J., *Abateregga Kun Namlondo ya Buganda* (History of the Baganda Kings), London, 1959.

Katate, A.G. and Kamugungunu, L., *Abagabe B'Ankole Ekitabo* (The Kings of Ankole) Kampala, 1955, being the oral traditions of Ankole.

Katoke, I., "Karagwe: A Pre-Colonial State", *Journal of World History*, 13, 1971.

Katoke, I., *The Karagwe Kingdom*, East Africa Publishing House, Nairobi, 1975.

Katumba, Ahmed and Welbourn, F.B. "Muslim Martyrs of Uganda", *Uganda Journal* 28/2 (1964).

Kimambo, I.N., "The Interior Before 1800" in I.N. Kimambo and A.J. Temu (eds.), *A History of Tanzania*, East African Publishing House, Nairobi, 1969.

Kitakule D. W., 'Bassekabaka Abataano Abasooka Kintu' (*The Five Pre-Kintu Kings*) Ebifa (1907-10).

Kayizzi, D.M., *Kabaka Daudi Chwa: Obulamu bwo mulembe Gwe Nebirowozo bye*, Kampala, Baganda Press, 1947.

Kiwanuka, M.S.M., 'Bunyoro and the British: a reappraisal of the decline and fall of an African Kingdom', *Journal of African History* 9/4 (1968), 603-619.

Kiwanuka, M.S.M., 'The Empire of Bunyoro-Kitara: Myth or Reality?' *Journal of African Studies* 2/1 (1968) 27-48: reprinted as Makerere History Papers No. 1, Kampala, Longmans of Uganda, 1968.

Kiwanuka, M.S.M., *A History of Buganda*, Longman, London, 1971.

Kiwanuka, M.S.M., ed. *The Kings of Buganda*, Nairobi, East African Publishing House, 1971.

Kiwanuka, M.S.M., "Nationality and Nationalism: The Buganda Case", mimeo, n.d.

Kiwanuka, M.S.M., 'Sir Apolo Kaggwa and the Pre-colonial History of Buganda', *Uganda Journal* 30/2 (1966), 137-52.

Kiwanuka, M.S.M., *A History of Buganda from the Foundation of the Kingdom to 1900*, London, 1971.

Kizito Tobi, W., 'The History of the Pre-Kintu Period, and the Origins of Kintu'in *Munno*, 1915 and 1916.

Konczacki, Z.A. & J.M. (eds.), *An Economic History of Black Africa*, Frank Cass, London, 1977.

Laclau, H.E., "Feudalism and Capitalism in Latin America", *New Left Review*, No. 67, May-June, 1971.

Langdale-Brown, I., "The Vegetation of Buganda", Memoirs of the Research Division, Dept. of Agriculture, Uganda Protect., Series 2. No. 2, 1959.

Lanning, E.C., 'Notes on the History of Kooki', *Uganda Journal* 23/2 (1959), 162-72.

Lawerence, J.C.D., "A Pilot Scheme for Grant of Land Titles in Uganda", *Journal of African Administration*, 12, 3, July, 1960.

Lee, J.M., "Uganda's First Year of Independence", *The Political Science Quarterly*, Vol. 35, 1964.

Lemarchand, *Rwanda and Burundi* Praeger Publishers, N.Y. 1970.

Lind, E.M., 'The Natural Vegetation of Buganda', *Uganda Journal* 20/1 (1956), 13-16.

Limqueco, P. and McFarlane, B., *Neo-Marxist Theories of Development*, St. Martin Press, N.Y. 1983.

Low, A.D., 'The Advent of Populism in Buganda', *Comparative Studies in Society and History* 30/4 (1964.

Low, A.D., 'British Public Opinion and the Uganda Question' October-December, 1892, *Uganda Journal* 18/2 (1954).

Low, A.D., *The Impact of Christianity in Tropical Africa*, London, 1967.

Low, A.D., 'The Northern Interior, 1840-1884', in *History of East Africa*, 1963.

Low, A.D., 'The British and Uganda, 1862-1900', unpublished Ph.D. thesis, Oxford, 1957. Kept in Rhodes House Library, Oxford.

Low, A.D., and Pratt, *Uganda and the British Overrule*, London, 1960.

Lubogo, Y.K., *A History of Busoga*, Nairobi, East African Literature Bureau, 1960 (English trans. by the Bantu Committee).

Lugard, F.D., *The Rise of Our East African Empire*, London, 1893, 2 vols.

Lugard, F.D., *British East Africa and Uganda*.

MacCall, D.F., *Africa in Time Perspective*, New York, Oxford University Press, 1960.

MacDermott, P., *British East Africa or the IBEA*, London, 1, 1893, N.e.. 1895.

Mafeje, A., "The Ideology of Tribalism", JMAS, 9, 2, 1970.

Mafeje, A., "The Land Question and Agrarian Revolution in Buganda" in W. Arens (ed.), *A Century of Change in Eastern Africa*, Mouton, The Hague, 1976.

Mafeje, A., "Neocolonialism, State Capitalism, or Revolution" in P. Gutkind and P. Waterman (eds.), *African Social Studies*. Heinemann, London, 1977.

Mafeje, A., "On the Articulation of Modes of Production", *Journal of Southern African Studies*, 8, 9, 1981.

Mafeje, A., "African Peasants: A Historical Anomaly?", *Africa Development*, X, 3, 1985.

Mafeje, A., "Dynamics of Land Tenure in Africa", *Ceres*, FAO, Rome, 1987.

Mafeje, A., "The Impact of Land Changes and Agrarian Policies on Common Property Resources in Africa", FAO, Rome, 1989.

Mair, L., *African Kingdoms*, Clarendon Press, Oxford, 1977.

Mair, L., *An African People in the Twentieth Century*, London, 1934.

Mair, L., "Clientship in east Africa", *Cahiers d' Etudes Africaines*, 2, 2, 1961.

Mair, L., *Primitive Government*, London (Pelican), 1962.

Mair, L., 'Buganda Land Tenure', *Africa*, 6/2, 1932

Mamdani, M., *Politics and class Formation in Uganda*, Monthly Review Press, New York, 1976.

Maquet, J., *The Premise of Inequality in Ruanda*, OUP, London, 1961.

Mazrui, A.A., & Engholm, G.F., "Violent Constitutionalism in Uganda", *Government and Opposition*, 2, 4, July-October, 1967.

McDonald, A.S., 'The Nature of Subsistence Agriculture in the Arable Areas of Uganda', mimeo, 1965.

Meillassoux, C., "La Phenomene Economique dans le societes traditionalles d'autosubsistence", CEA, 4, 1960, (published in English in 1978).

Meillassoux, C., *Anthropologie economique des Gouro be Cote d'Ivoire*, Mouton, The Hague, 1964.

Meillassoux, C., "Elaboration d'un modele socio-economique en ethnologie", *Epistemologie sociologique* 1-5, 1965.

Meillassoux, C., "From Reproduction to Production", *Economy and Society*, 1, 1, 1972.

Meillassoux, C., "The Social Organization of the Peasantry: The Economic Basis of Kinship", *Journal of Peasant Studies*, 1, 1, 1973.

Middleton, J., & Tait, D., *Tribes Without Rulers*, London, 1958.

Miti, James Kibuka Kabazzi, 'A Short History of Buganda, Bunyoro, Busoga, ANkole and Toro'; translated into English by G.K Rock. (Available in MSS form Makerere and University of London Libraries).

Morris, H.F., *A History of Ankole*, Nairobi, 1960.

Mukasa, Om. Ham., 'Some Notes on the Region of Mutesa', *Uganda Journal* 1/2 (1934) 116-33; 2/1 (1935) 60-70 (in Luganda with English translation).

Mukasa, Om. Ham., *Simudda Nyuma* (Go Forward), London, 1938. 2 Vols. A history of the region of Mutesa.

Mukwaya, A.B., *Land Tenure in Uganda: Present Day Tendencies*, East African Institute of Social Research, East African Studies, No. 1, 1959.

Mungonya, Z.K., 'The Bacwezi in Ankole', *Uganda Journal* 22/1 1958).

Nabudere, D.W., *Imperialism, the Politics of Class Formation and the National Question in Uganda*, mimeo, Dar es Salaam, 1976.

Nabudere, D.W., *Imperialism and Revolution in Uganda*, Onyx Press, London, 1980.

Nabwiso-Bulima, F., 'The Evolution of the Kyabazingaship of Busoga', *Uganda Journal* 30/2 (1966).

Nove, A., "On Reading Andre Gunder Frank", *The Journal of Development Studies*, 10, 3-4, April-July, 1974.

Nsimbi, M.B., *Amanya Amaganda Ne Nonno Zaago* (Kiganda names and their origins), Nairobi, East African Literature Bureau, 1959.

Nyakatura, J., *Abakama ba Bunyoro-Kitara* (The Traditional History of the kings of Bunyoro), Canada, 1947, 304 pp.

Nyakatura, J., *Anatomy of an African Kingdom*, Doubleday, NY, 1973.

Nyakatura, J., *Abakama ba Bunyoro*, trans. by T. Muganwa, ed. G. Uzoigwe, Anchor Books, Garden City, NY, 1973.

Nyakatura, J., *Aspects of Bunyoro Customs and Traditions*, trans by Z. Rigby, East African Literature Bureau, Nairobi, 1971.

Nyakatura, J., *Bunyoro Customs and Traditions*, East African Literature Bureau, Nairobi, 1978.

Oberg, K., 'The Kingdom of Ankole in Uganda", in *African Political Systems*, ed. M. Fortes and E. Evans-Pritchard, London, 1955.

Ocampo, J., "What's New and Old in the Theory of Imperialism", *Latin American Perspectives*, 4, Spring, 1975.

Ogot, B.A., *The Southern Luo*, Nairobi, East Africa Publishing House, 1967.

Oliver, R., *African History for the Outside World: An Inaugural Lecture Delivered on 13 May 1964*, London, 1964.

Oliver, R., 'Ancient Capital Sites in Ankole', *Uganda Journal* 23 (1959).

Oliver, R., 'The Baganda and the Bakonjo', *Uganda Journal* 18/1 (1954).

Oliver, R., *The Missionary Factor*, London, 1954: reissued 1965.

Oliver, R., 'A Question about the Bacwezi', *Uganda Journal* 17/2 (1963).

Oliver, R., 'The Royal Tombs of Buganda', *Uganda Journal* 23/2 (1959).

Oliver, R., 'The Traditional Histories of Ankole, Buganda and Bunyoro', *J. Roy. Anthrop. Inst.* (1958).

Oliver, R., (ed) *The Dawn of African History*, London, 1968.

Oliver, R., (ed) *The Middle Age of African History*, London, 1967.

Oliver, R., and Mathew, G., eds. *History of East Africa*, Vol. I, Oxford University Press, 1963 (vol. II 1965) (Abb. History of East Africa).

Oxaal, I., et al. *Beyond Sociology of Development*, Routledge and Kegan Paul, London, 1975.

Patnaik, U., et al. *Studies in the Development of Capitalism in India*, Vanguard Books Ltd, Lahore, 1978.

Pere, J.M., *L'Ouganda, la Mission Catholique, et les Agents de la Comagnie Anglaise*, Paris, 1893.

Perham, M., and Simmons, J., *Anthology of African Exploration*, London, 1951.

Pirouet, L., 'Baganda Evangelists', unpublished Ph.D; Thesis submitted in University of East Africa, 1968.

Pitman, C.R.S., 'The Mabira Forest', *Uganda Journal* 1/1 (1934).

Popper, K., *Conjectures and Refutations*, Routledge & Kegan Paul, London, 1963.

Portal, Sir Gerald H., *The British Mission to Uganda*, London, 1893.

Posnansky, M., 'Kingship, archaeology and historical myth', *Uganda Journal* 30/1 (1966).

Powesland, P.G., "History of Migration in Uganda", in A.I. Richards (ed), *Economic Development and Tribal Change*, W. Heffer & Son, Cambridge, 1954.

Powesland, P.G., *Economic Policy and Labor* (ed. W. Elkan); East African Studies, No. 10, 1957.

Pratt, R.C., "Nationalism in Uganda", *Political Studies*, Vol. 9, 1961.

Radwanski, S.A., "The Soils and Land Use of Buganda", Memoirs of the Research Division, Dept of Agriculture, Uganda, Series 1, No. 4, 1960.

Raper, A.B., and Ladkiln, G.R., 'The Banakalanga of Kyaggwe', *Uganda Journal* 15/2 (1951), 144-58.

Rey, P.P., *Colonialisme, Neo-Colonialisme et Transition au Capitalisme*, Maspero, Paris, 1971.

Rey, P.P., *Les Alliances des Classes*, Maspero, Paris, 1973.

Rey, P.P., "The Lineage Mode of Production", *Critique of Anthropology* 3, 1975.

Richards, A.I., *The Changing Social Structure of a Ganda Village*, Nairobi, East African Publishing House, 1966.

Richards, A.I., "Constitutional Problems in Uganda", *The Political Quarterly*, 33, 4 October-December, 1962.

Richards, A.I., *East African Chiefs*, Faber & Faber, London, 1959.

Richards, A.I., 'Social Mechanisms for Transfer of Political Rights in Some African Tribes', *Journal of the Royal Anthropological Institute* (1960), pp. 175-87.

Richards, A.I., et al, *Subsistence to commercial Farming in Present-day Buganda*, Cambridge univ. Press, 1973.

Rigby, P., *Persistent Pastoralists*, Zed. London, 1985.

Roberts, A., 'The Lost Countries of Bunyoro', Uganda Journal 26/2 (1962).

Roberts, A.D., 'The Sub-imperialism of the Baganda', *Journal of African History*, 18 (1963).

Rodney, W., *How Europe Underdeveloped Africa*, Tanzania Publishing House, 1972.

Roscoe, J., *The Baganda*, Cambridge, 1911, Reprinted London, Kegan Paul, 1966.

Roscoe, J., *Bakitara or Bunyoro: The First Part of the Report of the Mackie Ethnological Expedition to Central Africa*, Cambridge, 1923.

Roscoe, J., *The Banyankole: The Second Part of the Report of the Mackie Expedition*, Cambridge, 1924.

Roscoe, J., *The Bagesu: The Third Part of the Mackie Expedition*, Cambridge, 1924.

Rowe, J., *Lugard at Kampala*, Makerere History Paper No. 4 (1969.

Rowe, J., 'Myth, Memoir and Moral Admonition: Luganda Historical Writing, 1893-1939', *Uganda Journal* 33/1 (1969).

Roxborough, I., *Theories of Underdevelopment*, McMillan Press Ltd., London, 1979.

Salim, A.I. (ed.), *State Formation in Eastern Africa*, Heinemann, London, 1984.

Schapera, I. (ed.), *The Bantu-speaking Tribes of South Africa*, Routledge & Kegan Paul, London, 1937.

Schapera, I. (ed.), *Government and Politics in Tribal Societies*, Watts, London, 1956.

Sekamwa, L., ed. *Ekitabo Ky'empeewo* (History of the Oribi Antelope Clan), Kampala, 1905.

Sekiti, Lawi (On the Origins of Kintu and the Pre-Kintu Period), *Munno* (1915, 1916).

Skeens, S.R. 'Reminiscences of Busoga and its Chiefs', *Uganda Journal* 4/3, 1937.

Smith, Sheila, "Class Analysis versus World System: Critique of Samir Amin's Typology of Underdevelopment" in Limqueco, P. and McFarlane, B. (eds.), *Neo-Marxist Theories of Development*, St. Martin's Press, New York, 1983. Martin's Press, New York, 1983.

Stavenhagen, Rudolfo, "Seven Fallacies about Latin-America" in J. Petras and M. Zeitlin (eds), *Latin-America: Reform or Revolution?* Greenwich, N.Y., 1978.

Southail, Al *Alur Society*, London, 1956.

Southail, 'Alur Tradition and Its Historical Significance', *Uganda Journal*, 18/2 (1954).

Southwold, M., *Chieftainship and Bureaucracy in Buganda*, Nairobi and Kampala, East African Studies No. 1, 1953.

Southwold, M., 'The Inheritance of Land in Buganda', *Uganda Journal* 20/1 (1956).

Southwold, M., 'Succession to the Throne of Buganda', *in Succession to High Office*, ed. J. Goody (Cambridge Papers in Anthropology), Cambridge University Press, 1966.

Speke, J.H., *Journal of the Discovery of the Source of the Nile*, London and Edinburgh, 1863.

Stamp, L.D., "Natural Resources, Food and Population in Inter-Tropical Africa", Geographical Publications, England, 1956.

Stanley, H.M., *Through the Dark Continent*, London and New York, 1878, vol. II.

Stanley, R. and Neame, A. *The Exploration Diaries of H.M. Stanley*, London, 1961.

Steinhart, E., *Conflict and Collaboration*, Princeton University Press, Princeton, 1977.

Steinhart, E., "Herders and Farmers: The Tributary Mode of Production in Western Uganda" in Crummey, D. and Stewart, C.C. (eds), *Modes of Production in Africa*, Sage Publications, London, 1981.

Suret-Canale, J., "Les Sociétiés Traditionelles en Afrique Tropicale et le Concept de Mode de Production Asiatique", *La Pensée*, 117, 1964.

Suret-Canale, J., "Apropos du MPA", *La Pensee*, 142, 1968.

Taylor, J. "Neo-Marxism and Underdevelopment - A Sociological Fantasy", *Journal of Contemporary Asia* 4, 1, 1974.

Taylor, J.G., *From Modernization to Modes of Production*, MacMillan Press Ltd., London, 1979.

Taylor, J.V., *The Growth of the Church in Buganda*, S.C.M. Press, London, 1958.

Terray, E., *Marxism and 'Primitive' Societies*, Monthly Review Press, New York, 1972.

Thomas, H.B., 'Capax Imperi: The Story of Semei Kakungulu', *Uganda Journal* 5/1 (1937), 125-36.

Thomas, H.B., 'The Death of Bishop Hannington', *Uganda Journal* 8/1 (1940).

Thomas, H.B. & Spencer, A.E., *A History of Uganda Lands and Surveys*, Govt. Prenter, Entebbe, 1938.

Thomas, H.B. and Scott, R. *Uganda*, London, 1935.

Thomas, Kuhun, *The Structure of Scientific Revolutions*, University of Chicago Press, Chicago, 1962.

Tribe, K., "Political Change in Uganda", mimeo University of Essex, n.d.

Trowell M. & Wachsman, K., *Tribal Crafts of Uganda*.

Twaddle, M. "The Amin Coup", *Journal of Commonwealth Studies*, 10, 2, 1972.

Uzoigwe, G.N., "Pre-colonial Markets in Bunyoro-Kitara", *Comparative Studies in Society and History*, 14, 1972.

Vansina, J., *L'Evolution du royaume Rwanda des origines a 1900*, Brussels, 1962.

Vansina, J., *Oral Tradition*, London, 1965.

Vansina, J., 'African Kingdoms', *Africa* 14/3 (1962).

Vansina, J., 'Recording the oral History of the Bakuba: Methods and Results', *Journal of African History* 1/1 and 2.

Vansina, J., Maunay, R. and Thomas, L.V., eds. *The Historian in Tropical Africa*, London and Accra, 1964.

Villamil, J.J. (ed), *Transitional Capitalism and National Development: New Perspectives on Dependence*, The Harvester Press Sussex, 1979.

W.K. 'Abakama Ba Bunyoro-Kitara: The Kings of Bunyoro-Kitara', *Uganda Journal*: Part i 3/2 (1935) Part ii 4/1 (1936) Part iii, 5/1 (1937), 53-84.

Walker, H.W., *The Intelligencer* (Description of Mwanga in), Nov. 1888.

West, H.W., *Land Policy in Buganda*, Cambridge University Press, 1972.

West, H.W., *The Mailo System in Buganda*, Government Printer, Entebbe, 1964.

White Fathers, *The Geography Nensi Awamu*, White Fathers' Press, Bukalasa (Uganda), 1931.

Wild J.V., *The Story of the Uganda Agreement, 1900*, Nairobi, Eagle Press, 1949.

Willoughby, W.C., *The Soul of the Bantu*, London, S.C.M., 1928.

Wilson, C.T. and Felkin, R.W., *Uganda and the Egyptian Sudan*, London, 1882, 2 vols.

Winter, E.W., *Bwamba Economy*, East African Studies, No. 5, 1959.

Winter, E.W., *Beyond the Mountains of the Moon*, Routledge & Kegan Paul, London, 1959.

Wrigley, C., 'Buganda: An outline Economic History', *Econ. Hist. Rev.* 2nd ser. 10 (1957).

Wrigley, C., 'The Christian Revolution in Buganda', *Comparative Studies in Society and History* 2/1 (1959) 33-48.

Wrigley, C., *Crops and Wealth in Uganda*, East African Studies, No. 5, 1959.

Wrigley, C., 'Kimera', *Uganda Journal* 23/1 (1959).

Wrigley, C., 'Some Thoughts about the Bacwezi', *Uganda Journal* 22/1 (1958).

Zimbe, B.M. *Buganda Ne Kabaka* (Buganda and the King), Kampala, 1938.

Zwanenberg Van, R.M.A. & King, A., *An Economic History of Kenya and Uganda,* McMillan London, 1975.

INDEX

dynasty 26, 27
  in Ankore 50
  status 38, 114
Bahuma 19-20, 21, 30
  in Bunyoro 48, 50
  in Buzinza 28
  co-existence with Bairu 22, 24
  dynasty 19, 20
  political power 22-3
  status 24-5, 43, 69
Bahutu 14, 60
  labour dues 73
Bairu 14, 19, 21-2
  in Ankore 50, 51-2
  and Bahuma 22, 24
  in Buhaya 27
  in Buzinza 28
  defined 31
  ethnicity of 112
  labour dues 73
  and state power 52
  status 38, 55, 71
    political 24-5
  in Toro 49
Baker, 19
Balandier, G. 105
Balibar, E. 15-17
banana cultivation 77
Bantu 17, 18, 22, 50
  chiefdoms 40
Batoro *see* Toro
Batutsi 14, 22, 53, 74
  in Buha 29
  dynasty 41, 42, 113
  ethnicity 56-7
  in Rwanda 58, 59, 60
  status 38, 72
  see also Bahuma
Batwa in Rwanda 58, 60
beans 78
Beattie, J. 19-20, 21, 22, 24, 25, 26
  on Bahuma 47-8
  on feudalism 69-70
Belgian colonialism 114
Bonte, P. 71, 127
bourgeoisie 96

see also petit-bourgeoisie
British colonialism 35, 114
  and political organization 42, 43
  and trade 82-3
  see also colonialism
Buganda 30, 37
  bureaucracy 121
  development 79-80
  dynamism 101
  history 49
  Kabaka 105, 132-3, 135, 137
  land in 97, 99, 132-3
    and colonialism 133-6, 137-47
    control 67, 72
    fight for 133-4
  language 14
  origin of 31, 32-3, 34-5
  political organization 34-5, 61-3
  as single-ethnic kingdom 47, 61-3
  social formation 18
    and colonialism 132-49
  trade 80-1, 82, 100
Buha 17, 26
  dynamism 101
  as multi-kingdom 37, 38
  political organization 41
  social formation 18, 29
  tribal economy 75
Buhaya 17, 18
  class 114
  dynamism 101
  history 26, 27-8
  land in 97, 99
    control 44-5
  language 14
  as multi-kingdom 37, 38
  patronage 75-6
  political organization 22, 41, 43-4
  power in 45-6
  status 110
Buhutu 55-6
  power of 54, 55
Bunyoro 14, 17, 45, 101
  Bahuma in 48
  bureaucracy 50
  and Busoga 35

cattle 69
class 114
history 23-6, 47
land in 68-9, 97, 99
  control 72
as multi-ethnic 47
political organization 37
power in 48
ruling dynasties 19-22
social formation 18
status 110
trade 80-1, 100
bureaucracy/bureaucracies 121
and Bahuma 47-8
and kinship 39, 42
and lineage 46, 52, 59
modern 148
rise of 44
and tribute 63
Burundi 14, 17, 18
Bahima in 24
land in 97
as multi-ethnic 47
patronage 73, 74
political organization 22, 53
ruling dynasties 53-5
social stratification 57-8
stagnation 101
status 114
as unitary kingdom 37
Busoga 17, 30
land in 68, 97
language 14
as multi-kingdom 37
origin of 31, 33-4, 35
political organization 41, 46
social formation 18
trade 80-1
Busukuma 14
Busulu and *Envujjo* Law (1928) 136,
  138-9
Butoro *see* Toro
Buzinza 17
history 26, 28
language 14
as multi-kingdom 37, 38

political organization 22, 41
social organization 18, 19, 28-9, 43
trade 81, 100
tribal economy 75
Bwamba 17

C
capitalism 5, 147-8
and agriculture 109
and class struggle 95
development of 7
impact of 80, 83
inevitability of 111
as necessary 84, 116, 124, 149
and pastoralism 102
Cardoso, F.H. 4
cash crops 109, 128, 136, 138, 139
types of 83
cassava 77
caste 18, 38, 42, 56-7
  see also unitary kingdoms
cattle 127
accumulation 69, 70
as power 52, 99
rights over 72
as status 61, 69, 78, 114
chiefdoms 38, 43
and patron-client relationship 70
and royal dynasties 54
and tenants 67-8
Chilver, E.M. 87
Chwezi kings 20
class 109
in Buganda 68
and colonialism 5
and dependency 7
and exploitation 109-10
as inchoate 125
and patronage 119
in Rwanda 60
societies 11, 18, 57
and status 110-11, 112, 115
struggle 16, 94, 95-7
  and colonialism 146
in West Africa 104, 105
clients *see* patron-client relationship